HAMSTER
CARE FOR BEGINNERS

The Complete Family Guide to Choosing, Caring For, and Understanding Your Pet

HAMSTER CARE FOR BEGINNERS: *The Complete Family Guide to Choosing, Caring For, and Understanding Your Pet*

Copyright © 2025 by Dylanna Press

All rights reserved. No part of this publication may be reproduced, distributed, or transmitted in any form or by any means, including photocopying, recording, or other electronic or mechanical methods, without the prior written permission of the publisher, except in the case of brief quotations embodied in critical reviews and certain other noncommercial uses permitted by copyright law.

Disclaimer: The information contained in this book is for educational purposes only and is not intended as a substitute for professional veterinary care. While every effort has been made to ensure the accuracy of the information presented, the author and publisher assume no responsibility for errors, omissions, or any outcomes related to the use of this information. Always consult with a qualified veterinarian for medical advice regarding your pet's health.

The advice and strategies contained herein may not be suitable for every situation. This work is sold with the understanding that the author and publisher are not engaged in rendering veterinary, medical, or other professional services. If professional assistance is required, the services of a competent professional should be sought.

ISBN: 978-1-64790-439-5
Publisher: Dylanna Press
First Edition: 2025
Printed in the United States of America
10 9 8 7 6 5 4 3 2 1

For information about special discounts for bulk purchases, please contact:

Dylanna Publishing, Inc.
www.dylannapublishing.com

Contents

Introduction   5

Chapter 1: Is a Hamster Right for You?   9

Chapter 2: Setting Up Your Hamster's Dream Home   18

Chapter 3: Bringing Your Hamster Home   28

Chapter 4: Understanding Your Hamster   37

Chapter 5: Feeding Your Hamster Right   46

Chapter 6: Handling and Bonding   56

Chapter 7: Keeping Your Hamster Healthy   66

Chapter 8: Daily, Weekly, and Monthly Care   77

Chapter 9: When Problems Arise   83

Chapter 10: Growing Together   92

Quick Reference & Emergency Guide   99

Index 101

Introduction: Your Hamster Adventure Begins Here!

Are you thinking about getting a hamster? Maybe you've already fallen in love with one at the pet store, or perhaps your family is trying to decide if a hamster would be the right pet for you. Either way, you've come to the right place!

This book is written especially for kids like you (ages 10 and up) and your parents who want to provide amazing care for a hamster. We know you're smart enough to handle real information about pet care, and we respect that you want to do things right from the very beginning.

Why This Book Is Different

Unlike other pet guides that talk down to kids or overwhelm families with complicated advice, this book treats you like the capable, caring person you are. We'll give you the honest truth about hamster ownership—both the wonderful parts and the challenging parts—so you can make great decisions and provide excellent care.

You'll learn everything you need to know to:

- Choose the right hamster species for your family
- Set up a habitat that makes your hamster truly happy
- Develop daily care routines that work with your busy life
- Recognize and solve problems before they become serious
- Build a strong, trusting relationship with your pet
- Handle the entire journey from adoption through your hamster's senior years

What Makes a Great Hamster Owner?

Great hamster owners aren't born knowing everything - they're made through learning, practice, and genuine care for their pets. The best hamster families share a few important qualities:

They're committed learners who understand that good pet care requires knowledge and preparation, not just good intentions.

They're realistic planners who think through the time, space, and money required for proper hamster care before bringing their pet home.

They're patient observers who take time to understand their individual hamster's personality, preferences, and needs.

They're problem-solvers who stay calm during challenges and seek help when they need it.

Does this sound like you and your family? If so, you're already on the path to becoming an excellent hamster owner!

How to Use This Book

This book is designed to grow with you throughout your hamster ownership journey. You might read it cover-to-cover before getting your hamster, or use it as a reference guide when questions arise. Either approach works perfectly!

Each chapter builds on the previous ones, but they're also designed to stand alone when you need specific information quickly.

A Note to Parents

While this book is written primarily for young readers, it's designed to be a valuable resource for the entire family. Children ages 10-13 can understand and implement most of the care information with appropriate adult supervision and support.

Remember that regardless of your child's enthusiasm and commitment, parents remain ultimately responsible for pet welfare. This book will help you understand what that responsibility entails while supporting your child's growth as a pet caregiver.

Your Journey Starts Now

Hamster ownership is an incredible opportunity to develop responsibility, learn about animal behavior, and experience the joy of caring for another living being. It's also a chance to create lasting family memories and discover just how amazing these small animals can be.

Whether this is your first pet or an addition to your family's menagerie, approaching hamster care with knowledge, preparation, and genuine commitment sets you up for years of rewarding experiences.

Are you ready to become the kind of hamster owner that every hamster deserves? Let's begin this amazing journey together!

Ready to start? Chapter 1 will help you determine if a hamster is truly right for your family, while giving you realistic expectations about what hamster ownership actually involves. Let's make sure you're prepared for success from day one!

Chapter 1: Is a Hamster Right for You?

1.1 Meet the Amazing Hamster

Have you ever watched a hamster stuff its cheeks so full of food that it looks like it's got tiny balloons in its mouth? Or seen one run on its wheel like it's training for the Olympics? If you're reading this book, you've probably already fallen in love with these amazing little animals.

Hamsters aren't just cute pets—they're really interesting animals with their own personalities, amazing athletic skills, and cool social behaviors. Unlike many pets that sleep when you're awake, hamsters come alive in the evening, ready to entertain you with their acrobatic tricks and curious exploring.

> **FUN FACT**
> *Hamsters are part of the rodent family, just like mice, rats, and squirrels.*

What makes hamsters such special pets? They're the perfect size for gentle holding, they don't need walks like dogs, and they won't knock over your favorite things like cats might. But maybe most importantly, they give you something really special: the

Real Hamster Success Stories

Emma (Age 11, Massachusetts): *"I was nervous about getting a pet because I'd never had one before. But when I met Coco at the shelter, she was so calm and gentle. Now she's been my best friend for two years. She knows my voice and comes to the front of her cage when I get home from school. Taking care of her has taught me so much about responsibility."*

The Johnson Family (Parents with 8 and 10-year-old sons): *"We wanted a pet that would teach our boys about commitment without overwhelming our busy schedule. Our Syrian hamster, Peanut, has been perfect. The boys have learned to maintain his habitat, plan his meals, and even track his health. It's been an incredible learning experience for the whole family."*

chance to watch a wild animal's natural behaviors up close in your own home.

The Daily Wonder of Hamster Life

Each evening, as the sun goes down and your house gets quiet, your hamster's day begins.  You'll find out that these small animals have big personalities. Some are natural athletes who can run for miles on their wheels. Others are like little architects, spending hours moving their bedding to make perfect nests. Many are tiny comedians, finding creative ways to use their toys that will make you laugh out loud.

Watching your hamster's nightly routine becomes really relaxing for many families. There's something really satisfying about seeing your pet do well, explore, and act like the natural animal they are in the safe, comfortable home you've made for them.

Did You Know? A hamster can run up to 5 miles in a single night on their exercise wheel—that's like a human running a marathon!

1.2 Hamster Species Made Simple

Not all hamsters are created equal! While pet stores often display them together, different hamster species have very different needs, personalities, and care requirements. Let's meet the main types you'll encounter and help you figure out which might be the best fit for your family.

Syrian Hamsters: The Gentle Giants

Syrian hamsters (also called Golden hamsters) are the teddy bears of the hamster world. At 5-7 inches long and weighing 3-5 ounces, they're the largest pet hamster species and often the best choice for first-time hamster families.

Why families love Syrian hamsters: Syrian hamsters have calmer temperaments and are generally more tolerant of handling and less likely to bite. Their larger size makes it easier to spot health changes, and each Syrian hamster has distinct quirks and preferences. They typically live 2-3 years with proper care, with some reaching 3-4 years in exceptional cases.

Syrian hamster varieties come in many different colors and coat types.

- **Golden hamsters** have the classic honey-colored fur that gave them their name.
- **Teddy Bear hamsters** are long-haired Syrians with fluffy, soft fur that needs gentle brushing.
- **Panda hamsters** have black and white coloring that looks like a tiny panda bear.
- **Cinnamon hamsters** show warm brown coloring with gray underneath.

Dwarf Hamsters: The Tiny Acrobats

Dwarf hamsters are about half the size of Syrians, measuring 2-4 inches long and weighing 1-2 ounces. They're incredibly active and entertaining to watch, but they require more careful handling due to their small size and quick movements.

The three main dwarf species you'll see in pet stores are quite different from each other.

- **Campbell's Dwarf Hamsters** are the most common, with gray-brown fur and a dark stripe down their back. They're social and active but can be nippy if not handled regularly.
- **Winter White Dwarf Hamsters** are also called Siberian hamsters because they have the amazing ability to change from gray to white fur in winter, though this rarely happens under normal house lighting.
- **Roborovski Hamsters** are the smallest and fastest of all pet hamsters.

They're incredibly fun to watch but work best for families who enjoy watching more than handling.

Which Type Might Be Right for Your Family?

Choose a Syrian hamster if this is your first hamster experience, you have younger children who want to handle their pet, you want a calmer and more predictable companion, or you have space for a larger habitat since Syrians need more room.

Choose a dwarf hamster if you have experience with small pets, you mainly want to watch rather than handle your pet, you have limited space though they still need good-sized habitats, or you enjoy watching very active, acrobatic behaviors.

> **FUN FACT**
> Dwarf hamsters can fit through holes smaller than a quarter

Important note: Regardless of species, all hamsters are **solitary animals** and must be housed alone. Pet stores sometimes house them together when they're young, but adult hamsters will fight and can seriously injure each other.

1.3 The Hamster Commitment Check

Before you fall completely in love with the idea of hamster ownership, let's have an honest conversation about what you're committing to. This isn't meant to discourage you—it's designed to ensure you're prepared for success.

Time: Your Daily and Weekly Investment

Daily commitment (15-20 minutes):

- Morning check-in: Fresh water, quick health observation (5 minutes)
- Evening interaction: Feeding, gentle handling or observation (10-15 minutes)
- Spot cleaning: Removing soiled bedding from food/water areas (5 minutes)

Weekly commitment (30-45 minutes):

- Thorough cage cleaning: Complete bedding change, toy cleaning, habitat maintenance

- Health monitoring: Weighing, checking for any changes in behavior or appearance
- Supply management: Restocking food, bedding, and treats

Space: What Your Hamster Really Needs

Minimum habitat requirements:

- **Syrian hamsters:** 600 square inches of floor space (40-gallon long tank minimum)
- **Dwarf hamsters:** 450 square inches of floor space (29-gallon long tank minimum)
- **Bedding depth:** At least 6 inches deep for natural burrowing behavior
- **Placement:** Quiet area away from direct sunlight and temperature extremes

Beyond the habitat, you'll need space for: Supply storage for food, bedding, and cleaning supplies, temporary housing during cleaning, and a veterinary carrier for transport.

Financial Reality: Setup and Ongoing Costs

Starting costs for a proper hamster setup include a good-sized habitat, bedding for deep burrowing, an exercise wheel that fits your hamster properly, food and water supplies, hideouts and toys for mental stimulation, and a first veterinary checkup. Plan to spend about as much as a decent bicycle for the complete initial setup.

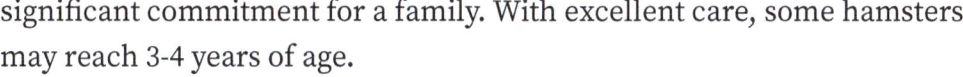

Monthly costs include fresh food, clean bedding, occasional veterinary care, and new toys or enrichment items. This usually costs about the same as a family pizza night each month.

The 2-3 Year Journey

Hamsters typically live 2-3 years, which might seem short compared to dogs or cats, but represents a significant commitment for a family. With excellent care, some hamsters may reach 3-4 years of age.

For children: Your pet will be with you through important developmental years. A hamster adopted in 3rd grade will likely be a companion through 5th or 6th grade.

For families: You're committing to consistent care through seasons, school years, vacations, and family changes.

Family Readiness Assessment

Physical readiness:

- Can family members lift and carry a 20-30 pound habitat for cleaning?
- Are children old enough to handle a small, quick-moving animal gently?
- Does anyone in the household have allergies to small animals or bedding materials?

Are You Ready? Interactive Family Checklist

Work through this checklist together as a family. Be honest—your future hamster depends on it!

Housing and Space

[ ] We have identified a suitable location for a hamster habitat

[ ] We have space for a proper-sized habitat (minimum 600 sq. inches for Syrian, 450 for dwarf)

[ ] We have a plan for deep bedding (6+ inches) and understand it needs weekly changing

[ ] We have considered noise levels (hamsters are most active at night)

Time and Commitment

[ ] Someone in our family is available for daily care (morning and evening check-ins)

[ ] We can commit to weekly deep cleaning (30-45 minutes every week)

[ ] We understand this is a 2-3 year commitment and are prepared for the full lifespan

[ ] We have a plan for vacation and emergency care

Financial Readiness

[ ] We have budgeted for initial setup costs (about the cost of a decent bicycle)

[ ] We can afford monthly ongoing expenses (about the cost of a family pizza night)

[ ] We have funds set aside for potential veterinary emergencies

[ ] We understand that costs continue even if interest decreases

Knowledge and Preparation

[ ] We have researched hamster care requirements (you're doing this now!)

[ ] We have located an exotic pet veterinarian in our area

[ ] We understand species differences and have chosen Syrian vs. dwarf

[ ] We have realistic expectations about handling, interaction, and hamster behavior

Family Agreement

[ ] All family members are on board with the decision

[ ] We have discussed primary caretaker responsibilities (usually the most interested child, with parent backup)

[ ] We understand that parents are ultimately responsible for the pet's welfare

[ ] We have discussed what happens if circumstances change (moving, allergies, loss of interest)

Emotional readiness:

- Are you prepared for the natural cycle of pet ownership, including end-of-life care?
- Can you provide consistent care even when the novelty wears off?
- Will you be able to find appropriate care during vacations or family emergencies?

What If You're Not Ready Yet?

If you didn't check every box, that's perfectly okay! It's much better to wait until you're truly prepared than to get a hamster and discover you're overwhelmed. Consider waiting until after a major family transition, until children are slightly older and more capable of consistent care, until you have more predictable schedules and routines, or until you've saved enough for both setup and emergency costs.

When You're Ready to Move Forward

If you checked all the boxes and feel confident about proceeding, congratulations! You're demonstrating the kind of thoughtful, responsible approach that leads to successful pet ownership.

Your next step is learning how to create the perfect home for your future hamster companion. In Chapter 2, we'll dive deep into habitat setup, showing you exactly how to create a space where your hamster can thrive and express their natural behaviors.

Remember: The families who do best with hamsters are those who approach pet ownership as a learning adventure rather than just acquiring a cute animal. Your hamster will teach you patience, responsibility, and the joy of caring for another living being. Are you ready for that incredible journey?

∙∙∙∙∙∙∙∙∙∙∙∙∙∙∙∙∙∙∙∙∙∙∙∙∙∙∙∙∙∙∙∙∙∙∙∙

Coming up in Chapter 2: Learn how to create your hamster's dream home with proper habitat setup, essential features, and smart shopping strategies that will save you money while ensuring your pet's happiness and health.

Chapter 2: Setting Up Your Hamster's Dream Home

2.1 Choosing the Right Home Size

Imagine living in a closet-sized room for your whole life. That's exactly what happens when hamsters are kept in homes that are too small. The most important decision you'll make for your hamster's happiness is choosing a home that gives them space to run, burrow, explore, and simply be a hamster.

Here's something many pet stores won't tell you: Most hamster cages sold in stores are too small. Those colorful plastic cages with tubes and rooms might look fun, but they often give less than half the space your hamster actually needs.

The Science Behind Space Requirements

Minimum space requirements based on current research:

Syrian hamsters: 600 square inches of continuous floor space (40-gallon long tank minimum)

Dwarf hamsters: 450 square inches of continuous floor space (29-gallon long tank minimum)

Why these numbers matter: In the wild, hamsters travel several miles each night looking for food. While we can't copy that exact experience, giving them enough space lets them do natural behaviors like walking around their territory, searching different areas for food, creating underground tunnels, and running in patterns that go beyond just wheel time.

FUN FACT

In the wild, a hamster's territory can span 8 miles

Modern Housing Options That Actually Work

Option 1: Glass Aquarium Tanks (Recommended for Beginners)

Glass aquarium tanks work great for beginners. You control air flow with mesh lids, they're escape-proof with no gaps or weak spots, they're easy to clean with smooth surfaces, you get great visibility to watch your hamster's natural behaviors, and bedding stays contained without messy spills around the habitat.

Recommended sizes:

- **40-gallon long tank:** Perfect for Syrian hamsters (36" x 18" = 648 sq inches)

- **29-gallon long tank:** Minimum for dwarf hamsters (30" x 12" = 360 sq inches)

- **75-gallon tank:** Ideal for those wanting extra space (48" x 18" = 864 sq inches)

Cost range: Medium-priced option - more than a simple bin cage but less than premium commercial cages

Option 2: Large Bin Cages (Budget-Friendly DIY)

Budget-friendly option that lets you create exactly what your hamster needs. Large bin cages cost much less than commercial cages, you can customize size and features, they're lightweight and easier to move for cleaning, and you can find supplies at most hardware stores.

How to create a safe bin cage: Choose clear plastic storage bins (110+ quart capacity), create ventilation by cutting large windows on opposite sides and cover with hardware cloth, secure the lid so it cannot be pushed off from inside, and smooth all edges by filing down any sharp plastic edges.

Safety warnings: Never use wire mesh smaller than ¼ inch (hamsters can get stuck), and ensure all ventilation holes are covered with secure screening.

Option 3: High-Quality Commercial Cages (Premium Choice)

What to look for: Deep base at least 6 inches deep for proper bedding, proper bar spacing of ¼ inch for dwarf hamsters and ½ inch maximum for Syrians, horizontal orientation that's long and wide rather than tall and narrow, easy access with large doors for cleaning and interaction, and solid construction with no wobbly parts or sharp edges.

Making the Size Decision

Consider your hamster's activity level: High-energy hamsters need every inch of the minimum space requirement, while senior hamsters still need proper space but may use it differently. Both Syrian and dwarf species benefit from generous habitats.

Future-proofing your setup: Growing hamsters will need adult-sized space within a few months, extra space allows for more toys and activities, and larger habitats are actually easier to keep clean.

2.2 Essential Home Features

Now that you understand space requirements, let's dive into the specific features that transform a simple container into a hamster paradise. Each element serves a crucial purpose in your hamster's physical and mental health.

The Foundation: Proper Bedding Depth

Why 6+ inches matters: In the wild, hamsters live in extensive burrow systems that can extend 2-3 feet underground. While we can't replicate that depth, providing 6-8 inches of bedding allows for natural burrowing behaviors that are essential for mental health.

Best bedding materials:

- **Aspen shavings** provide excellent burrowing ability with low dust and natural odor control

- **Paper-based bedding** works well for hamsters with respiratory sensitivities

- **Hemp bedding** offers super absorbent qualities and is virtually dust-free

Avoid these bedding types: Cedar or pine shavings contain oils that can cause respiratory problems. Fluffy bedding can cause blockages if eaten. Corn cob bedding molds easily and can cause internal blockages.

Exercise Wheels: Getting the Size Right

Proper wheel sizing:

- **Syrian hamsters:** 8-11 inch diameter minimum
- **Dwarf hamsters:** 6.5-8 inch diameter minimum

Why size matters: A wheel that's too small forces your hamster to arch their back unnaturally, which can cause spinal problems over time. The wheel should be large enough that your hamster's back stays straight while running.

Wheel features to prioritize: Look for solid running surfaces with no bars or mesh that can catch feet, quiet operation with ball bearings or quality construction for silent spinning, easy cleaning with removable parts for thorough washing, and stable bases that won't tip over during enthusiastic use.

Multi-Chamber Hideouts: Creating Security

Why hiding spots are essential: Hamsters are prey animals, which means they naturally need safe spaces where they can retreat when feeling vulnerable. Multiple hideouts give them options and help reduce stress.

Hideout requirements: Multiple entrances allow escape routes and prevent trapped feelings. Appropriate sizing means large enough to turn around in but cozy enough to feel secure. Use natural materials like wood or ceramic rather than plastic that can be chewed. Easy cleaning with removable tops or wide openings for maintenance is important.

Strategic hideout placement: Place one near the food area for comfortable eating, one in the opposite corner for sleeping and nesting, and one near the water source for security while drinking.

Water and Food Systems

Water bottles vs. water dishes: Both can work, but each has advantages. Water bottles keep water clean and prevent spills, but must be checked daily for clogs. Water dishes provide more natural drinking positions but can get contaminated with bedding.

Food storage solutions: Use a ceramic bowl that can't be tipped over for dry food, provide an easy-to-clean surface for vegetables and treats, and create foraging opportunities by scattering feeding to encourage natural behavior.

2.3 Creating the Perfect Environment

Beyond the basic necessities, creating the perfect hamster environment involves understanding the subtle factors that impact your pet's health and happiness.

Temperature and Climate Control

Ideal temperature range: 65-75°F (18-24°C)

Why temperature matters: Hamsters are sensitive to temperature extremes and can enter torpor (a hibernation-like state) if conditions get too cold below 60°F (15°C), which can be dangerous for pet hamsters. Temperatures above 80°F (27°C) can cause heat stress.

Seasonal considerations: Summer requires providing cooling options like

ceramic tiles and ensuring good ventilation. Winter needs avoiding drafts and considering room heating if the house gets cold. Keep habitats away from direct air conditioning flow, and never use heat lamps or heating pads as they create fire hazards.

Lighting and Ventilation

Natural daylight cycles: Hamsters are most active at dawn and dusk and throughout the night. Proper lighting helps maintain their natural body rhythms.

Ventilation essentials: Poor air circulation leads to ammonia buildup from urine, which can cause respiratory problems and stress. Provide air flow from multiple directions for cross-ventilation while ensuring gentle air movement rather than direct drafts.

Enrichment That Makes a Difference

QUICK TIP
Keep cages away from direct sunlight and cold drafts.

Mental stimulation essentials: Ceramic or wooden tunnels provide exploration opportunities. Sand baths with chinchilla sand help with grooming, especially for dwarf hamsters. Hidden food encourages natural foraging behavior. Wooden platforms and safe branches offer climbing structures. Extra-deep bedding sections allow for extensive digging.

Enrichment rotation: Change toys and accessories weekly to maintain interest. Use seasonal themes with natural materials that change throughout the year. Try DIY options like cardboard boxes, toilet paper tubes, and brown paper bags.

2.4 Shopping Smart: Essential vs. Nice-to-Have

Setting up a hamster habitat can quickly become expensive if you're not strategic about your purchases. Let's break down what you absolutely need versus what would be nice additions.

> ### Essential Items Checklist ✅
> **Must-have items before bringing your hamster home:**
>
> - **Housing:** Proper-sized habitat (40-gallon tank or equivalent commercial cage), secure lid with mesh and clips or weighted edges, and bedding with 2-3 bags of quality material for initial deep layer.
>
> - **Exercise and Activity:** Exercise wheel in proper size for your hamster species, at least 2 multi-chamber hiding spots, and water bottle or dish with daily refill capability.
>
> - **Food and Nutrition:** High-quality hamster food in 1-2 pound bag, ceramic or glass tip-resistant food bowls, and healthy treats for bonding and training.
>
> - **Emergency/Health:** Small pet carrier for transport, kitchen scale for monitoring weight changes, and basic first aid supplies as recommended by your vet.

Nice-to-Have Additions

Items that enhance quality of life but aren't immediately necessary:

Enrichment Upgrades: Sand bath container especially for dwarf hamsters, multi-level climbing platforms for exploration, puzzle feeders and treat dispensers for foraging, and ceramic or wooden tunnels and tubes for exploration systems.

Convenience Items: Cage-specific cleaning tools, storage containers for food and bedding organization, timer systems for consistent feeding schedules, and backup equipment like extra water bottles and spare wheels.

> **QUICK TIP**
> *Rotate toys and tunnels every week to prevent boredom.*

Money-Saving Strategies That Work

Homemade hideouts can be made from cardboard boxes that are free and replaceable, coconut shells that are natural and durable, or wooden boxes you can build in custom sizes.

Bulk purchasing: Buy bedding in bulk when on sale, purchase larger food bags while checking expiration dates, and share bulk purchases with other hamster families.

Seasonal shopping: Take advantage of back-to-school sales that often include pet supplies, post-holiday clearance for storage containers and accessories, and end-of-season sales to stock up on supplies.

Budget-Friendly Setup Plans

Starter setup (Budget-friendly): 40-gallon tank from hardware store, mesh lid with clips, aspen bedding (3 bags), basic exercise wheel, ceramic food bowl, water bottle, cardboard hideouts (free), and basic hamster food.

Mid-range setup (Balanced): Quality commercial cage, premium bedding, silent spinner wheel, multi-chamber hideout, ceramic food and water dishes, premium hamster food, basic enrichment items, and veterinary carrier.

Remember: investing in quality setup from the beginning saves money and stress in the long run. Your hamster's health and happiness are worth doing it right the first time.

···

Coming up in Chapter 3: Learn the step-by-step process of bringing your hamster home, from choosing the right individual to those crucial first weeks of adjustment and trust-building.

Chapter 3: Bringing Your Hamster Home

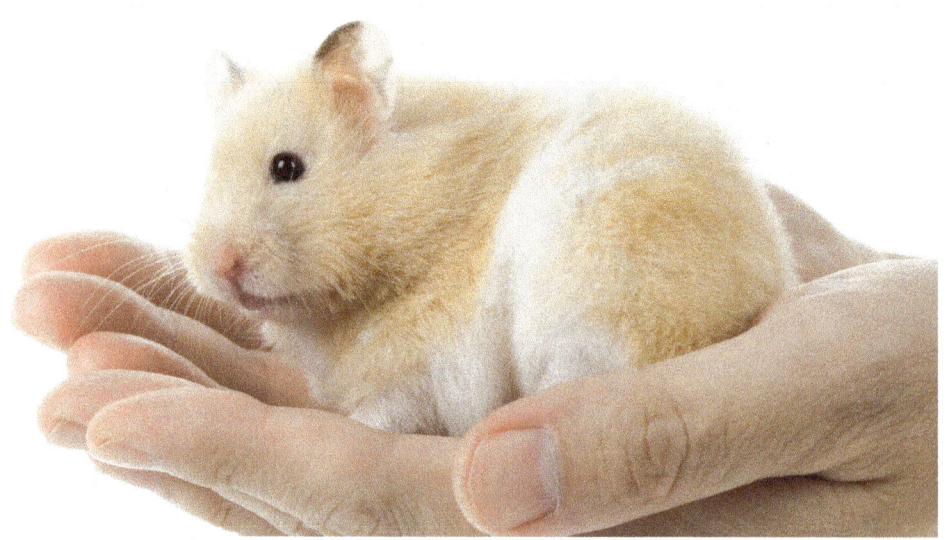

3.1 Choosing Your Hamster

The moment you've been preparing for has arrived—it's time to choose your hamster! This decision will shape your family's experience for the next 2-3 years, so let's make sure you know exactly what to look for and what questions to ask.

What a Healthy Hamster Looks Like

Physical health indicators: Bright, clear eyes with no discharge, cloudiness, or excessive tearing. Clean, dry nose that should be slightly moist but not runny. Full, glossy coat with no bald patches, excessive scratching, or dull appearance. Proper body weight that's not too thin with ribs showing or overweight with difficulty moving. Clean bottom with no signs of diarrhea or wetness around the tail area.

Behavioral health signs: Alert and curious hamsters show interest in surroundings and new people. Normal movement means no limping, head tilting, or coordination problems. Appropriate activity level shows they're active during evening hours if you're viewing at the proper time. Responsive to stimuli means they react appropriately to sounds and movement. Comfortable with gentle approach means they don't panic when you move slowly near the enclosure.

▶ **Red flags to avoid:** Lethargy or excessive sleeping, especially during evening hours. Labored breathing, wheezing, mouth breathing, or unusual sounds. Wet tail, which is a serious condition requiring immediate veterinary attention. Aggressive behavior with excessive biting or defensive posturing. Repetitive behaviors like constant bar chewing or pacing.

Age Considerations

Young hamsters (6-8 weeks): Advantages include easier socialization and quick adaptation to new environments. Considerations include requiring more frequent feeding and being more fragile during handling. Best for families with time for daily gentle interaction.

Adult hamsters (3-12 months): Advantages include established personality, easier handling, and more predictable behavior. Considerations include possibly taking longer to bond with a new family. Best for families wanting a more settled, predictable pet.

Senior hamsters (18+ months): Advantages include often being very gentle, grateful for good care, and offering special bond potential. Considerations include shorter remaining lifespan and possible developing health issues. Best for experienced families or those wanting to provide rescue care.

Species-Specific Selection Tips

For Syrian hamsters: Individual personality matters since each Syrian has distinct traits. Size can vary as some are naturally larger or smaller within the normal range. Coat length options include short-haired, long-haired, and satin varieties. Choose color preferences based on your family's likes.

For dwarf hamsters: Activity level varies as some are naturally more active than others. Size is more consistent with less variation within species. Social history is important—know if they've been housed alone properly. Handling tolerance varies as some dwarf hamsters are more tolerant of handling than others.

> **FUN FACT**
> Hamsters can recognize their owners by scent within just 3-4 days!

3.2 Where to Find Your Hamster
Reputable Sources

Animal shelters and rescues: Advantages include often having health history, adult personalities established, and supporting animal welfare. Ask about previous owner history, known health issues, and temperament observations. Cost is usually a modest adoption fee. Best for families wanting to provide a second chance.

Ethical breeders: Advantages include known genetics, health testing, and early socialization. Look for clean facilities, health guarantees, and breeding records. Cost varies depending on variety. Best for families wanting specific traits or maximum lifespan.

Pet stores (choose carefully): Advantages include convenience, usually younger animals, and immediate availability. Evaluate store cleanliness, staff knowledge, and animal care standards. Cost varies typically. Best for families needing immediate availability with proper store vetting.

Questions to Ask Any Source

Health and history: "What do you know about this hamster's health history?" "Has this hamster been seen by a veterinarian?" "What food and bedding has this hamster been using?" "How long has this hamster been available for adoption?"

Behavior and temperament: "How does this hamster typically react to handling?" "What time of day is this hamster most active?" "Has this hamster shown any behavioral concerns?" "How social is this hamster with people?"

QUICK TIP
Hamsters are nocturnal. Shop late in the day to see them awake and active

Care requirements: "What specific care needs does this hamster have?" "Are there any special dietary requirements?" "What supplies do you recommend for this individual?" "Do you offer any health guarantees or return policies?"

Red Flags at Any Source

Facility concerns: Overcrowded conditions, strong odors or dirty enclosures, multiple sick animals, staff with poor knowledge of hamster care, and unwillingness to answer questions.

Individual hamster concerns: Housed with incompatible species, signs of fighting or stress, improper diet or housing, reluctance to allow handling observation, and no health information available.

3.3 The Journey Home

The trip from adoption location to your home is your hamster's first major stress test. How you handle this transition sets the tone for your entire relationship.

Safe Transport Essentials

Proper carrier requirements: Large enough for hamster to stand and turn around, adequate airflow without drafts, escape-proof latches and solid construction, small amount of familiar bedding from original location, and stability so it won't slide around in car or tip over.

QUICK TIP
Prepare your hamster's cage before bringing them home.

What to bring for transport: Carrier with secure lid—never use cardboard boxes. Small amount of familiar bedding for comfort and scent familiarity. Water bottle or dish for longer journeys over 1 hour. Small amount of food in case of unexpected delays. Towel for covering to reduce visual stress during transport.

Travel Tips for Stress Reduction

In the car: Secure placement with carrier on floor or held securely, never on seats. Temperature control by avoiding direct sunlight, air conditioning, or heating vents. Quiet environment by minimizing loud music, talking, or sudden noises. Smooth driving by avoiding sudden stops, sharp turns, or aggressive acceleration. Short duration by taking the most direct route home.

For longer journeys: Plan rest stops every 2-3 hours for water and observation. Bring backup supplies including extra bedding, food, and water. Have emergency contacts with veterinarian info for destination area. Consider overnight stops if journey exceeds 6 hours.

Preparing for Arrival

Final habitat check: Ensure room is 65-75°F, provide dim and calm lighting conditions, maintain quiet environment for initial adjustment, have food, water, and bedding prepared, and brief family about the quiet adjustment period.

Initial placement: Choose quiet location away from household traffic and noise. Include any bedding or toys from previous location. Set up observation spot where you can watch without disturbing. Keep emergency supplies and carrier accessible for potential vet visits.

3.4 The First Week: Adjustment Period

The first week is crucial for your hamster's successful transition. This period requires patience, consistency, and careful observation rather than enthusiastic interaction.

Days 1-2: Arrival and Initial Settling

Your hamster's perspective: Everything is new and potentially threatening. Your hamster needs time to assess their environment and determine that it's safe.

Your role: Provide minimal interaction by observing from a distance. Give consistent care by providing food and water quietly. Respect hiding by allowing extensive hiding without interference. Monitor health by watching for eating, drinking, and elimination.

Normal first-day behaviors: Extensive hiding may occur as they might not emerge for 12-24 hours. Limited eating happens as stress can reduce initial appetite. Restlessness might include nervous exploration or pacing. Startled responses mean overreaction to normal household sounds.

Concerning behaviors that need attention: No water consumption after 24 hours, no food consumption after 36 hours, labored breathing or any difficulty breathing, injury signs like limping, bleeding, or obvious pain, and extreme lethargy or being unresponsive to gentle stimuli.

QUICK TIP
Don't poke or pet. Let your hamster explore the cage on their own.

Days 3-4: Exploration and Routine Development

What you'll notice: Increased movement with more confident exploration of habitat. Feeding patterns as they establish preferred eating times. Territorial behavior as they claim specific areas for different activities. Curiosity about you as they may approach when you're near.

Your activities: Use gentle voice by speaking softly when near the habitat. Maintain consistent timing by feeding and providing water at same times daily. Practice passive observation by watching and learning their preferences. Respect boundaries by not forcing interaction.

Routine establishment: Feeding schedule with morning and evening provisions. Activity periods by noting when your hamster is most active. Preferred areas by observing sleeping, eating, and exercise locations. Stress indicators by learning your hamster's specific stress signals.

Days 5-7: First Gentle Interactions

When your hamster is ready: Approaches habitat front showing curiosity about your presence. Eating normally with consistent food and water consumption. Active exploration using all areas of habitat confidently. Calm body language with relaxed posture and normal grooming.

Beginning interaction: Hand feeding by offering small treats through cage bars. Gentle talking using consistent, calm voice. Slow movements avoiding sudden gestures or sounds. Respect refusal—if hamster retreats, give more time.

Signs of successful adjustment: Normal eating patterns with consistent food consumption. Regular activity including wheel usage, exploration, and grooming. Curiosity about humans by approaching when you're near. Stress reduction with less hiding and more confident movement.

Building Trust Foundation

Trust-building activities: Consistent presence by spending quiet time near habitat daily. Predictable routine with same feeding and care schedule. Positive associations where gentle voice equals food or treats. Respect for boundaries by never forcing interaction.

QUICK TIP
Offer small treats by hand. Gently place a treat in the cage to begin bonding.

Avoid these trust-breaking mistakes: Sudden movements or quick gestures near habitat. Loud noises including shouting, sudden sounds, or chaos. Forced handling by grabbing or cornering your hamster. Inconsistent care with irregular feeding or attention. Punishment—never scold or punish a hamster.

When to Seek Help

Veterinary concerns: Prolonged eating refusal over 48 hours. Respiratory problems like wheezing or labored breathing. Injury signs including limping, bleeding, or swelling. Behavioral extremes like excessive aggression or lethargy. Elimination problems including diarrhea, straining, or no output.

Behavioral consultation: Excessive fear after one week of consistent care. Aggression issues with biting that doesn't improve. Destructive behavior including excessive chewing or habitat damage. Sleep disruption with constant activity or excessive sleeping.

Week One Success Indicators

Physical health: Steady weight without losing weight rapidly. Normal elimination with regular, formed droppings. Clear eyes and nose without discharge or cloudiness. Active periods with regular exercise and exploration.

Behavioral adjustment: Reduced hiding by spending time in open areas. Normal grooming with regular self-cleaning behavior. Curiosity showing interest in new sounds or movements. Routine establishment with predictable daily patterns.

By the end of the first week, your hamster should be showing clear signs of adjustment and beginning to develop trust with your family. This foundation will make the next phase—active bonding and relationship building—much more successful.

Remember: Every hamster adjusts at their own pace. Some are confident within days, while others need weeks to fully settle. The key is consistency, patience, and reading your individual hamster's signals.

Coming up in Chapter 4: Learn to understand your hamster's body language, communication signals, and daily rhythms so you can build a deeper relationship and provide better care.

Chapter 4: Understanding Your Hamster

4.1 Hamster Body Language: Reading the Signs

Learning to read your hamster's body language is like learning a new language—one that will make your relationship so much better and help you take better care of your pet. Hamsters talk to us all the time through how they move and act, but most people miss these important signals.

Happy and Confident Hamster Signals

Relaxed body posture is what you see when your hamster feels safe and happy. When your hamster feels good, their ears point forward with curious interest rather than fear. Their breathing stays steady and quiet through their nose, and their fur lies smooth and flat against their body. A happy hamster stands normally on all four feet with their tail in a natural position rather than tucked under their body or puffed up with stress.

Positive exploration behaviors show a hamster who feels safe in their environment. You'll see active nose twitching as they check out their surroundings, with whiskers pointing forward during exploration. A confident hamster walks with steady steps without hesitation, comfortably climbing and stretching to use all parts of their habitat. Regular grooming sessions are especially important signs of comfort, as hamsters only do this when they feel completely safe.

QUICK TIP
Watch the ears. Ears forward = alert or curious. Ears back = nervous or resting.

Social engagement signals show that your hamster is beginning to recognize and trust you. A hamster ready for friendship typically approaches the front of their habitat when you appear, demonstrating curiosity rather than fear. They may stand on their hind legs to investigate something interesting, or engage in gentle nibbling of your fingers as a form of soft exploration. The ultimate sign of trust occurs when your hamster feels secure enough to eat while you're nearby.

Stress and Fear Indicators

Defensive postures emerge when hamsters feel threatened or unsafe. Their ears flatten back against their head, signaling fear or defensive mode. The fur along their back may stand up in a response called piloerection, which makes them appear larger and more intimidating. A stressed hamster crouches low to the ground with their body ready to flee at a moment's notice, while their tail gets pulled close to their body for protection.

Stress behaviors include excessive hiding and refusing to come out even for food, repetitive movements like pacing, bar chewing, or constant wheel running, freezing and becoming completely motionless when approached, excessive grooming that can indicate stress, and aggressive posturing with lunging or striking without actual contact.

Fear responses include rapid breathing with fast, shallow breaths through the mouth, trembling with visible shaking, escape attempts with frantic trying to get away, vocalizations like squeaking, hissing, or chattering sounds.

Warning Signs to Take Seriously

Illness indicators include lethargy with unusual inactivity or slow movement, hunched posture with rounded back indicating pain or discomfort, labored breathing with difficulty breathing or mouth breathing, discharge from eyes, nose, or other body openings, and balance problems like stumbling, head tilting, or coordination issues.

Pain signals include reluctance to move and staying in one position, guarding behavior by protecting specific body parts, unusual vocalizations like crying, whimpering, or distress calls, changes in eating with difficulty chewing or swallowing, and altered grooming where they're unable to clean normally.

4.2 Daily Rhythms and Natural Behaviors

Understanding your hamster's natural daily schedule is really important for giving good care and building a strong friendship. Hamsters are most active at dawn and dusk and throughout the night, which means their schedule is quite different from yours.

Natural Activity Patterns

Evening wake-up typically happens between 6 and 8 PM as your hamster slowly comes out of their sleeping areas. This time begins with grooming as they clean themselves and get ready for the day ahead. You'll see them carefully checking their habitat and marking their territory with their scent. The first big meal of the day usually happens during this time.

> **QUICK TIP**
> Flattening their body = fear. If your hamster presses flat to the ground, they're trying to hide in plain sight.

Peak activity (9 PM - 2 AM): This is when you'll see intensive exercise with heavy wheel running and climbing, major feeding with their largest meal and food hoarding, exploration as they investigate all areas of habitat, nest maintenance with rearranging bedding and territories, and the most interactive period, which is the best time for human interaction.

Daytime rest (6 AM - 5 PM): Deep sleep periods with extended rest in preferred hideouts, occasional stirring with brief wake-ups for water or bathroom, minimal activity with very quiet movements if any, nest time for comfortable resting in bedding, and recovery period for physical and mental restoration.

Working with Your Hamster's Schedule

Best interaction times: Early evening (7-9 PM) is the gentle wake-up period. Prime time (9 PM-12 AM) is when they're most receptive to handling and play. Late evening (12-2 AM) finds them active but possibly less social. Avoid daytime except for essential care or health checks.

Feeding schedule alignment: Primary feeding should happen at 7-8 PM as hamster becomes active. Secondary feeding works well at 10-11 PM during peak activity. Fresh foods should be given in evening only and removed within 24 hours.

4.3 Natural Behaviors: What's Normal and Why

Understanding what behaviors are natural and instinctive helps you provide appropriate enrichment and recognize when something might be wrong.

Burrowing and Nesting Instincts

Why hamsters burrow: Temperature regulation keeps underground areas cooler in summer and warmer in winter. Predator protection provides tunnels as escape routes and hiding spots. Food storage creates underground chambers for hoarding supplies. Comfort and security come from enclosed spaces that reduce stress and anxiety.

Normal burrowing behaviors: Deep digging creates tunnels in bedding. Multiple chambers provide separate areas for sleeping, eating, and waste. Continuous maintenance includes regular tunnel repair and expansion. Bedding collection involves gathering material for nest construction.

Providing for burrowing needs: Adequate bedding depth requires minimum 6 inches, preferably 8-10 inches. Burrowing-friendly materials include aspen shavings and paper-based bedding. Multiple hide boxes in various sizes and styles help. Tunnel accessories like ceramic or wooden tunnels work well. Digging boxes with separate containers and extra-deep substrate provide enrichment.

Hoarding and Food Storage

Why hamsters hoard: Survival instinct involves preparing for times when food is scarce. Seasonal behavior shows increased storage during winter months. Comfort activity means hoarding provides psychological security. Territorial marking happens as food storage areas become scent-marked territories. Natural foraging mimics wild food-gathering behavior.

QUICK TIP
Don't wake a sleeping hamster. Waking suddenly can make them panic and bite. Let them wake on their own.

Normal hoarding behaviors: Cheek stuffing fills cheek pouches to capacity. Transport patterns involve carrying food to specific storage areas. Sorting behavior organizes different food types. Protective storage hides food in secure locations.

Supporting healthy hoarding: Scatter feeding hides food around habitat for foraging. Variety of foods provides different textures and types to sort. Storage spaces offer multiple hiding spots for food caches. Regular cleaning removes spoiled stored food weekly.

Grooming Rituals

Complete grooming sequence:

1. Paw cleaning with licking paws and cleaning face

2. Ear cleaning using damp paws to clean ears

3. Body grooming by licking and cleaning fur systematically

4. Tail cleaning with thorough cleaning of tail and hindquarters

Why grooming is important: Hygiene maintenance removes dirt, food particles, and odors. Scent management distributes natural oils and personal scent. Stress relief happens as grooming releases endorphins and reduces anxiety.

4.4 Hamster Communication: Sounds and Signals

FUN FACT
Hamsters can hear higher frequencies than dogs. They pick up on sounds we can't — even the squeak of electronics.

Hamsters communicate through various sounds, scents, and body language. Learning to recognize and interpret these signals will help you understand your hamster's needs and emotional state.

Vocal Communications

Happy sounds: Soft chirping indicates contentment, often during eating or grooming. Quiet squeaking shows mild excitement or curiosity. Purring sounds demonstrate deep contentment, similar to cat purring. Gentle clicking indicates satisfaction, often during food enjoyment.

Neutral sounds: Sniffing represents normal investigation and scent gathering. Mild squeaking indicates general communication or mild interest. Quiet vocalizations are routine sounds during daily activities. Breathing sounds are normal respiratory noises during activity. Movement sounds are typical noises from walking and climbing.

Warning and stress sounds: Loud squeaking indicates fear, pain, or strong protest. Hissing represents defensive warning, telling others to stay away. Chattering teeth shows anger or extreme stress. Crying sounds indicate distress, pain, or fear.

When to be concerned: Continuous vocalization with ongoing distress calls. Respiratory sounds like wheezing, rattling, or labored breathing. Pain vocalizations including crying or whimpering during movement. Aggressive sounds with escalating hissing or screaming. Sudden silence when a normally vocal hamster becomes quiet.

Understanding Your Hamster's Signals to You

Signs of recognition: Approaching when you appear shows recognizing your presence. Calm behavior during care shows accepting routine maintenance. Food acceptance means taking treats from your hand. Reduced hiding indicates feeling secure in your presence. Curiosity about you shows investigating your scent and voice.

FUN FACT
Hamsters rely on smell more than sight. They use scent to recognize you, their cage, and even their toys.

Trust indicators: Grooming in your presence shows comfort enough for vulnerable activities. Sleeping near habitat front indicates feeling secure with you nearby. Gentle nibbling represents exploratory behavior, not aggressive. Relaxed body language shows normal posture when you're around. Vocalizations to you indicate communicating directly with you.

Requesting behavior: Standing at habitat front indicates asking for attention or food. Persistent gentle sounds show trying to communicate needs. Following your movement means tracking your location. Increased activity when you're present shows excitement about interaction.

Responding Appropriately to Communication

When your hamster is happy: Continue current activities—you're doing something right. Give gentle reinforcement with soft voice and calm presence. Maintain routine since consistency supports continued contentment.

When your hamster shows stress: Reduce stimulation by lowering noise, dimming lights, and decreasing activity. Give space by allowing retreat and hiding time. Evaluate environment by checking for stressors or changes. Maintain basic care by continuing feeding and cleaning quietly. Monitor health since stress can indicate underlying problems.

When your hamster seems to be communicating needs: Assess basics including food, water, cleanliness, and temperature. Consider timing—are you responding to natural rhythms? Evaluate enrichment to see if your hamster needs more stimulation. Check health since communication could indicate discomfort.

Understanding your hamster's communication transforms your relationship from basic caretaking to genuine companionship. Each hamster has their own personality and communication style, so spend time observing and learning your individual pet's unique signals.

Coming up in Chapter 5: Learn everything about proper hamster nutrition, from choosing the right commercial food to safe treats and foods to avoid completely.

Chapter 5: Feeding Your Hamster Right

5.1 Understanding Hamster Nutrition

Good nutrition is the foundation of your hamster's health, energy, and long life. Unlike dogs or cats, hamsters have very specific food needs that reflect their wild origins as desert animals that eat both plants and small amounts of meat.

What Hamsters Eat in the Wild vs. Captivity

In their natural habitat, hamsters are opportunistic feeders who spend most of their active hours looking for food. Their wild diet is mostly seeds, grains, and grasses, plus occasional insects, small amounts of plants, and even tiny amounts of meat when they can find it.

The key difference between wild and captive diets is variety and activity level. Wild hamsters might sample dozens of different seed types in a single night, while also burning tremendous energy through miles of foraging travel. Pet hamsters need us to provide appropriate variety within a controlled framework that matches their more sedentary lifestyle.

Commercial Food: Reading Labels and Choosing Quality

Understanding protein needs is really important when picking commercial hamster food. Adult hamsters need about 16-18% protein, while growing hamsters, pregnant females, and nursing mothers need 18-20% protein. Too little protein leads to poor fur condition, slow growth, and weak immunity. Too much protein can stress the kidneys and lead to weight gain in less active hamsters.

Carbohydrate content should make up the majority of your hamster's diet, ideally 45-65% of the total food. Look for complex carbohydrates from whole grains rather than simple sugars. Quality hamster foods list ingredients like oats, barley, wheat, and various seeds as primary components.

> **QUICK TIP**
> *Don't overfeed! 1–2 tablespoons per day is plenty for Syrian hamsters. Dwarfs need even less.*

Fat content needs careful balance at 4-7% for adult hamsters. Young, active, or pregnant hamsters can handle fat content on the higher end of this range, while older or less active hamsters benefit from the lower end.

Ingredient quality indicators separate premium foods from budget options. The first five ingredients should be recognizable whole foods like sunflower seeds, oats, barley, or wheat. Avoid foods that list "by-products," "meal," or generic terms like "grain products" as primary ingredients.

Pellet vs. seed mix debate: Pellets ensure balanced nutrition with every bite and prevent selective eating, where hamsters pick out favorite seeds and ignore nutritious but less appealing components. However, seed mixes provide mental stimulation through foraging behavior. Many experienced hamster owners find success with high-quality seed mixes supplemented with a small amount of pellets.

Feeding Schedules That Work

Timing feeds with natural rhythms maximizes your hamster's health and your family's convenience. Since hamsters are most active in the evening and throughout the night, their primary feeding should occur around 7-8 PM as they begin their daily activity.

Portion control prevents obesity while ensuring adequate nutrition. A good starting point is 1-2 tablespoons of food daily for Syrian hamsters, with dwarf hamsters requiring about 1-1.5 tablespoons. However, individual needs vary based on age, activity level, and metabolism.

Two-meal approach works well for many families. Provide the majority of food (about 70%) during the evening feeding, with a smaller portion (30%) available in the morning. This schedule accommodates natural eating patterns while ensuring food availability if your hamster wakes during the day.

Food freshness management prevents spoilage and maintains nutritional value. Check food dishes daily, removing any uneaten fresh foods after 24 hours. Dry food can remain available longer, but any food that becomes damp or develops an odor should be discarded immediately.

5.2 Fresh Foods and Healthy Treats

Fresh foods provide essential vitamins, minerals, and mental stimulation that even the highest quality commercial foods cannot fully replicate. However, introducing fresh foods requires knowledge of safe options, proper portions, and gradual introduction techniques.

Safe Vegetables and Portion Guidelines

Leafy greens form the foundation of healthy fresh food additions. Romaine lettuce, spinach, kale, and swiss chard provide excellent nutrition when offered in appropriate amounts. Start with pieces no larger than your hamster's paw, offered every other day initially.

FUN FACT
Broccoli is a superfood for hamsters. It's packed with vitamins and most hamsters love it — just serve in tiny pieces.

Root vegetables like carrots, sweet potatoes, and beets offer different nutritional profiles and textures. These should be offered in even smaller portions than leafy greens due to their higher sugar content. A thin slice of carrot or a small cube of sweet potato provides appropriate serving sizes.

Bell peppers of all colors offer vitamin C and satisfying crunch. Remove seeds and offer strips about the size of your hamster's ear. Red and yellow peppers tend to be sweeter and more readily accepted than green varieties.

Fruit Treats and Frequency

Fruit serves as dessert rather than dietary staple in hamster nutrition. The natural sugars in fruit provide quick energy and palatability, but excessive fruit consumption can lead to diarrhea, obesity, and dental problems. Limit fruit treats to twice weekly in very small portions.

Berries including blueberries, strawberries, and raspberries offer antioxidants in hamster-friendly sizes. One or two blueberries or a small strawberry piece provides an appropriate treat.

Apple and pear pieces should be offered without seeds, which contain compounds that can be harmful in large quantities. A thin slice about the size of your thumbnail provides adequate portion size.

Protein Treats and Timing

Occasional protein supplementation supports coat health, muscle development, and overall vitality, particularly for growing, pregnant, or recovering hamsters. However, too much protein can stress the kidneys and should be offered sparingly.

FUN FACT
Wild hamsters eat insects. They're omnivores! Tiny bits of cooked egg, chicken, or dried mealworms add healthy protein.

Cooked chicken or turkey provides high-quality protein when offered plain, without seasoning, oils, or skin. Cool completely before offering, and provide pieces no larger than your hamster's paw. Offer protein treats no more than twice weekly for adult hamsters.

Hard-boiled eggs offer complete protein with essential amino acids. Offer small pieces of white or yolk separately to determine preference. Never offer raw eggs due to salmonella risk.

Foraging and Enrichment Feeding

Scatter feeding mimics natural foraging behavior while providing mental stimulation. Instead of placing all food in a bowl, hide small portions throughout the habitat. This encourages natural searching behaviors and extends eating time, preventing boredom.

Puzzle feeders and treat-dispensing toys challenge your hamster's problem-solving abilities while making meals more engaging. Simple options include toilet paper tubes with ends folded closed or small boxes with holes cut for access.

Seasonal variety keeps meals interesting while taking advantage of fresh, local produce. Spring might feature fresh herbs like parsley or cilantro, while summer offers berries and melons. Fall brings squashes and root vegetables, while winter focuses on stored vegetables and occasional dried fruits.

5.3 Dangerous Foods: What to Avoid Completely

Understanding which foods can harm your hamster is just as important as knowing what to feed them. Some foods that are healthy for humans can be toxic or dangerous for hamsters due to their small size, different metabolism, and sensitive digestive systems.

Toxic Foods That Can Be Fatal ☠

Dangerous foods that can hurt your hamster include **chocolate**, which contains chemicals that are toxic to hamsters even in small amounts. **Onions and garlic** contain things that damage red blood cells in hamsters, leading to serious health problems. **Grapes and raisins** should be avoided as they've been linked with kidney problems in some small animals. Since no safe amount has been figured out, it's best to avoid these fruits completely.

Avocado contains persin, a compound that can cause digestive upset, difficulty breathing, and fluid buildup around the heart in small animals. All parts of the avocado, including the flesh, pit, and skin, should be avoided.

Raw beans and potatoes contain natural toxins that can cause serious illness. Green potatoes are particularly dangerous due to solanine content. Always cook these foods thoroughly before offering tiny amounts, though it's safer to avoid them entirely.

Foods That Cause Digestive Problems

Citrus fruits including oranges, lemons, limes, and grapefruits are too acidic for hamster digestive systems. They can cause mouth sores, stomach upset, and diarrhea.

Iceberg lettuce lacks nutritional value and can cause diarrhea due to its high water content and low fiber. Choose nutrient-dense alternatives like romaine lettuce or spinach instead.

Processed human foods including chips, crackers, cookies, and candy contain excessive salt, sugar, preservatives, and artificial ingredients that hamsters cannot process properly.

Dairy products cannot be properly digested by hamsters after weaning, as they lack the necessary enzymes to break down lactose. Milk, cheese, and yogurt can cause severe diarrhea and dehydration.

Raw meat and fish pose risks of bacterial contamination, parasites, and foodborne illness. Hamsters' digestive systems are not equipped to handle the bacteria naturally present in raw proteins.

Common Household Items That Are Dangerous ☠

Caffeinated beverages including coffee, tea, and sodas contain stimulants that can cause rapid heart rate, hyperactivity, and potentially fatal cardiac events in hamsters. Even small amounts can be dangerous.

Alcoholic beverages are toxic to hamsters and can cause depression of the central nervous system, difficulty breathing, and death. Never offer any amount of alcohol to your hamster.

Sugary treats designed for humans including candy, cookies, and sweetened cereals contain excessive sugar that can lead to diabetes, obesity, and dental problems. The artificial sweetener xylitol is particularly dangerous.

Salty snacks including pretzels, chips, and salted nuts contain dangerous levels of sodium that can cause dehydration, kidney problems, and high blood pressure in hamsters.

Signs of Food Poisoning and Emergency Response

Immediate symptoms of food poisoning include:

- Vomiting or diarrhea
- Lethargy or unusual tiredness
- Difficulty breathing
- Loss of coordination

These symptoms can develop within minutes to hours of eating toxic foods.

Emergency response involves removing any remaining toxic food, providing fresh water, and contacting your veterinarian immediately. Never wait to "see if they get better" when dealing with potential poisoning.

5.4 Special Dietary Considerations

Different life stages and health conditions require modifications to standard

hamster nutrition. Understanding these special needs helps ensure optimal health throughout your hamster's life.

Feeding Growing and Young Hamsters

Juvenile nutrition needs differ significantly from adult requirements. Young hamsters require 18-20% protein compared to 16-18% for adults, supporting rapid growth and development. They also need more frequent feeding, with food available at all times rather than scheduled meals.

QUICK TIP
Offer food at all times. Growing hamsters need constant access to food — don't limit portions early on.

Growth monitoring helps ensure proper development. Weigh young hamsters weekly, expecting steady weight gain until they reach adult size around 3-4 months.

Pregnancy and Nursing Nutrition

Increased protein requirements support fetal development and milk production. Pregnant and nursing females need 18-20% protein throughout gestation and lactation.

Unlimited food access becomes necessary during late pregnancy and throughout nursing. Remove portion restrictions and provide constant access to high-quality food.

Senior Hamster Nutrition

Easier digestion becomes important as hamsters age beyond 18 months. Softer foods, smaller pieces, and more frequent meals help senior hamsters maintain adequate nutrition despite potential dental or digestive challenges.

Weight management requires careful attention in senior hamsters. Some lose weight due to decreased appetite or difficulty eating, while others gain weight from reduced activity. Monitor body condition closely and adjust portions accordingly.

Hydration support becomes crucial as older hamsters may drink less water. Offer water-rich vegetables and ensure multiple water sources are easily accessible.

Managing Health Conditions Through Diet

Diabetes management requires eliminating high-sugar foods and providing consistent, measured meals. Work with your veterinarian to develop appropriate portion sizes and feeding schedules.

Digestive sensitivities may develop in some hamsters, requiring elimination of specific foods that cause upset. Keep detailed food diaries to identify triggers, and introduce new foods very gradually.

Understanding these special dietary needs ensures your hamster receives appropriate nutrition throughout their life, supporting health, longevity, and quality of life during every stage of development and aging.

•••

Coming up in Chapter 6: Learn safe handling techniques, bonding activities, and fun training exercises that will strengthen your relationship with your hamster while keeping both of you safe and comfortable.

Chapter 6: Handling and Bonding

6.1 Safe Handling Techniques

Learning to handle your hamster safely and confidently is one of the most important skills you'll learn as a hamster owner. Good handling keeps both you and your hamster comfortable while building the foundation for a trusting friendship. Most hamster bites happen because of wrong handling techniques rather than mean personalities.

The Foundation of Safe Handling

Understanding hamster bodies helps you give the right support during handling. Hamsters have flexible spines that can be hurt by wrong grips. They have delicate rib cages that can be squeezed by tight holding. They also have quick reflexes that can lead to unexpected movements. Their small size means they can be seriously hurt by falls as short as two feet.

Reading readiness signals prevents stressful handling sessions and reduces bite risk. A hamster ready for handling typically appears alert but calm, may approach the front of their habitat when you're near, and shows relaxed body language without defensive posturing. Never attempt to handle a hamster who is sleeping, eating, or showing signs of stress or illness.

Creating the right environment for handling success involves choosing appropriate timing, location, and preparation. Handle your hamster during their naturally active evening hours when they're alert and engaged. Choose a quiet area with minimal distractions, and always sit down or handle over a secure surface to prevent injury from accidental drops.

QUICK TIP
Scoop, don't grab. Use two hands like a scoop under their body. Never grab from above — it feels like a predator attack.

Step-by-Step Handling Process

Initial approach should be slow and predictable. Place your hand flat in the habitat, palm up, and allow your hamster to investigate at their own pace. Many hamsters will climb onto your hand voluntarily once they become comfortable with your scent and presence. This natural approach builds trust more effectively than grabbing or cornering.

Proper lifting technique involves supporting your hamster's entire body weight securely. Use both hands to create a safe "bowl" shape, with one hand supporting the chest and front legs while the other supports the hindquarters and back legs. Never grab a hamster by the scruff of the neck, tail, or individual limbs, as this can cause serious injury.

Secure holding position keeps your hamster feeling safe while preventing escapes. Hold them close to your body with hands cupped around them, leaving space for breathing while preventing jumping. Keep your movements slow and deliberate, as sudden motions can startle even well-socialized hamsters.

Safe return technique is just as important as proper lifting. Lower your hamster gradually back to their habitat, allowing them to step off your hands rather than dropping them. Many hamsters will jump from your hands when they're ready to return home, which is normal behavior that shouldn't be discouraged.

Handling Different Hamster Personalities

Confident hamsters who approach readily and seem comfortable with interaction can often be handled more frequently and for longer periods. These hamsters may enjoy brief exploration outside their habitat under supervision and often respond well to gentle training activities.

FUN FACT
Each hamster has a unique personality. Some are outgoing explorers, others are shy and prefer quiet snuggles.

Shy or nervous hamsters require extra patience and shorter handling sessions. Start with just a few minutes of contact and gradually increase duration as they become more comfortable. These hamsters often prefer predictable routines and may never enjoy extensive handling, which is perfectly normal.

Defensive hamsters who bite, hiss, or struggle extensively need special consideration. These behaviors often indicate fear rather than aggression, and forced handling will only increase their stress. Focus on building trust through feeding interactions and passive observation before attempting physical contact.

Senior hamsters may require modified handling techniques due to arthritis, decreased mobility, or increased fragility. Use gentler grips, shorter sessions, and provide extra support for their joints. Some elderly hamsters prefer being petted in their habitat rather than being lifted and moved.

When Not to Handle Your Hamster

Sleep disruption should be avoided except in true emergencies. Hamsters are naturally nocturnal and need uninterrupted daytime sleep for good health. Waking a sleeping hamster for handling can cause stress and may result in defensive biting.

Eating and drinking are times when hamsters prefer to be left alone. Interrupting meals can cause stress and may lead to food guarding behaviors. Wait until your hamster has finished eating before attempting interaction.

Illness or injury makes handling potentially harmful and certainly stressful. Sick hamsters need quiet rest and should only be handled when necessary for medical care. Consult your veterinarian about appropriate handling techniques for injured or ill hamsters.

Stress indicators signal that handling should stop immediately. These include rapid breathing, struggling to escape, vocalizations of distress, or defensive posturing. Return your hamster to their habitat immediately and try again later when they're calmer.

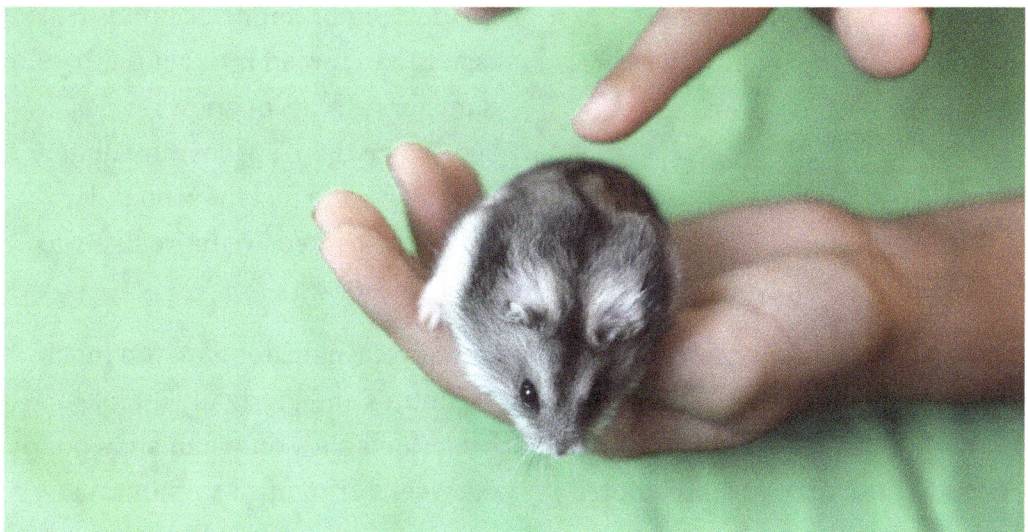

6.2 Building Trust and Bonding

Trust grows slowly through consistent positive interactions and respect for your hamster's boundaries. Unlike dogs or cats, hamsters don't naturally want human friendship, so building a bond takes patience and understanding of their unique social needs.

The Trust-Building Process

Establishing routine creates predictability that helps hamsters feel secure. Handle your hamster at the same time each day, use the same gentle voice, and follow consistent patterns in your interactions. This predictability helps reduce anxiety and allows your hamster to anticipate and prepare for handling sessions.

Positive associations link your presence with good things happening. Start by simply sitting near your hamster's habitat while they're active, speaking softly and offering treats through the bars. Over time, your hamster will begin to associate your voice and presence with positive experiences.

Respecting boundaries builds trust faster than forced interaction. If your hamster retreats or shows stress signs, give them space immediately. Hamsters who feel their boundaries are respected are more likely to choose interaction voluntarily in the future.

Gradual progression prevents overwhelming your hamster with too much too fast. Start with brief sessions of a few minutes and gradually increase duration as your hamster becomes more comfortable. Some hamsters bond quickly within days, while others may take weeks or months to fully trust.

Hand-Feeding for Trust Building

Treat selection should focus on high-value foods that your hamster finds irresistible. Small pieces of fresh fruit, sunflower seeds, or tiny bits of cooked chicken often work well. Use treats that are small enough to eat quickly so your hamster doesn't need to retreat to consume them.

Feeding technique involves offering treats on your flat palm rather than holding them

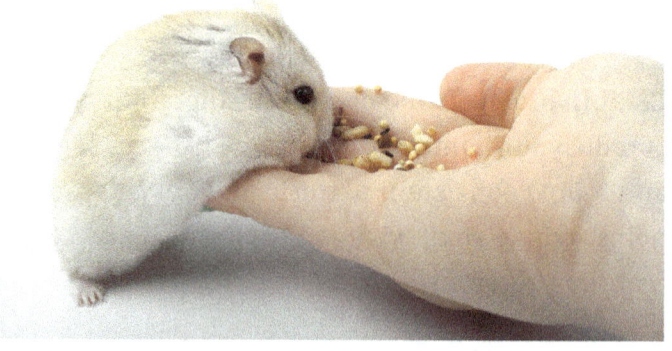

between your fingers. This prevents accidental finger bites and allows your hamster to approach at their own pace. Keep your hand steady and resist the urge to move toward your hamster.

Timing considerations work best during your hamster's natural feeding periods in the evening. A hungry hamster is more motivated to overcome mild anxiety for a desirable treat. However, never withhold regular food to make your hamster "hungrier" for treats.

Progressive challenges can gradually increase your hamster's comfort level. Start by offering treats through cage bars, then with the habitat door open, then with your hand inside the habitat, and finally during out-of-cage time. Each step should be mastered before moving to the next.

Voice and Movement Techniques

Gentle vocalization helps your hamster recognize and feel comfortable with your presence. Speak in low, soothing tones and use consistent phrases during interactions. Many hamsters learn to recognize their names and may respond to familiar voices.

QUICK TIP

Speak softly. Use a calm voice when near your hamster to help them associate you with safety.

Slow movements prevent startling your hamster and triggering defensive responses. Quick gestures can be perceived as threats, even by well-socialized hamsters. Practice moving deliberately and smoothly around your hamster's habitat.

Predictable patterns in your movements help your hamster feel secure. Approach from the same direction, use similar gestures, and maintain consistent body language. This predictability reduces anxiety and makes your hamster more likely to remain calm during interactions.

6.3 Simple Training and Enrichment

While hamsters aren't as trainable as dogs, they can learn simple behaviors and responses that make care easier and provide mental stimulation. Training should always be positive and reward-based, focusing on natural behaviors rather than complex tricks.

Basic Response Training

Name recognition is often the first and most useful training goal. Use your hamster's name consistently during feeding, handling, and positive interactions. Many hamsters learn to respond to their names within a few weeks of consistent practice.

QUICK TIP
Hamsters can learn routines! If you handle them gently at the same time each day, they'll start expecting and enjoying it.

Coming when called can be taught through positive reinforcement with treats. Start by calling your hamster's name when they're already moving toward you, then reward them with a treat. Gradually increase the distance and challenge level as they begin to associate their name with rewards.

Litter Training Basics

Natural tendencies make litter training easier than many people expect. Most hamsters naturally choose one or two corners of their habitat for elimination, making it relatively simple to place a litter box in these preferred areas.

Litter box setup should use hamster-safe litter materials like recycled paper or aspen shavings. Avoid clay or clumping litters, which can cause intestinal blockages if ingested. Place the litter box in the corner where your hamster naturally eliminates.

Positive reinforcement helps encourage litter box use. When you observe your hamster using the box correctly, offer verbal praise and occasional treats. Never punish accidents, as this can create stress and actually make training harder.

> ### Enrichment Through Training
>
> **Puzzle solving** provides mental stimulation while building problem-solving skills. Create simple puzzles using toilet paper tubes with treats inside, or hide food in different locations around the habitat. Start with easy challenges and gradually increase difficulty.
>
> **Obstacle courses** can be created using safe household items like cardboard boxes, toilet paper tubes, and small ramps. Encourage exploration with treats placed at various points along the course. This type of enrichment mimics natural exploration behaviors.
>
> **Foraging games** satisfy natural instincts while providing exercise. Hide treats throughout the habitat, scatter feeding instead of bowl feeding, or create "treasure hunts" with multiple hidden rewards. These activities can occupy your hamster for extended periods.
>
> **Interactive toys** that require manipulation provide ongoing mental stimulation. Puzzle feeders, treat-dispensing balls, and toys that can be moved or rearranged help prevent boredom and encourage natural behaviors.

6.4 Supervised Exploration and Playtime

Out-of-cage time provides valuable exercise and mental stimulation while strengthening your bond with your hamster. However, this activity requires careful preparation and constant supervision to ensure safety.

Setting Up Safe Play Areas

Room preparation involves hamster-proofing the space to prevent injury and escape. Remove or secure electrical cords, block access to small spaces where your hamster could become trapped, and eliminate any toxic plants or dangerous objects. Choose a room with a door that can be closed securely.

Boundary creation helps contain your hamster's exploration to a manageable area. Use cardboard panels, exercise pens designed for small animals, or clear storage containers to create defined play spaces. Ensure boundaries are at least 12 inches high to prevent jumping over.

Surface considerations affect both safety and cleanup. Hard floors like tile or hardwood are easier to clean but may be slippery. Carpeted areas provide better traction but can be difficult to clean if accidents occur. Consider using washable blankets or towels to create appropriate surfaces.

Enrichment additions make playtime more engaging and beneficial. Provide tunnels, hideouts, climbing structures, and toys that encourage natural behaviors. Rotate these items regularly to maintain interest and challenge.

QUICK TIP
Cardboard tunnels make great bonding tools. Let them crawl through tubes onto your hand or lap during playtime.

Supervision Techniques

Constant attention is essential during out-of-cage time. Hamsters can quickly get into dangerous situations, squeeze through surprisingly small spaces, or injure themselves on seemingly safe objects. Never leave your hamster unsupervised outside their habitat.

Positioning yourself strategically allows you to monitor your hamster while remaining unobtrusive. Sit at floor level where you can easily observe and reach your hamster if needed. Avoid standing over them, which can be intimidating.

Emergency preparedness involves knowing how to safely catch and return your hamster if they become frightened or try to escape. Keep a small towel or container nearby for safe capture, and know the location of potential hiding spots in your chosen room.

Returning to the Habitat

Ending signals help your hamster understand when playtime is finishing. Use consistent verbal cues and begin gathering toys or treats about five minutes before you plan to return them to their habitat. This preparation reduces stress and makes the transition smoother.

Gentle capture should be done calmly and confidently. Many hamsters will return to their habitat voluntarily if you leave the door open and place treats inside. If capture is necessary, use the same gentle handling techniques you've practiced during regular interactions.

Remember that not all hamsters enjoy or need extensive out-of-cage time. Some are perfectly content with a well-enriched habitat and minimal handling. Respect your individual hamster's preferences and never force activities that cause stress or fear.

Building a strong bond with your hamster takes time, patience, and respect for their individual personality. The investment in proper handling and trust-building pays dividends in easier care, reduced stress for both you and your pet, and a more rewarding relationship overall.

Coming up in Chapter 7: Learn to recognize signs of good health, understand common health problems, and know when to seek veterinary care to keep your hamster healthy throughout their life.

Chapter 7: Keeping Your Hamster Healthy

7.1 What a Healthy Hamster Looks Like

Learning to recognize the signs of good health in your hamster is one of the most important skills you can develop as a pet owner. Hamsters are prey animals, which means they naturally hide signs of illness to avoid attracting predators. This makes it really important for you to understand what normal, healthy hamster behavior and appearance look like.

Physical Health Signs

Bright, alert eyes are one of the best indicators of good health. A healthy hamster's eyes should be clear and shiny, without any discharge, cloudiness, or excessive tearing. The area around the eyes should be clean and dry, with no redness or swelling. Your hamster should blink normally and track movement with their eyes when they're awake.

Clean, dry nose shows proper respiratory function. A healthy hamster's nose should be slightly moist but not runny, with no discharge or crusting. While hamsters naturally have wet noses from constant sniffing, excessive moisture or colored discharge can indicate respiratory problems.

Glossy, full coat reflects good nutrition and overall health. Healthy hamster fur should lie smoothly against the body, feel soft to the touch, and have a natural shine. There should be no bald patches, excessive shedding, or matted areas. Different hamster breeds have varying coat textures, but all should appear well-groomed.

Good body condition means your hamster maintains an appropriate weight for their size and age. You should be able to feel their ribs with gentle pressure but not see them prominently. A healthy hamster has a rounded but not bulging belly, with no visible hip bones or spine. Their movements should be smooth and coordinated.

Normal breathing is quiet and regular. Healthy hamsters breathe through their nose without audible sounds, wheezing, or labored breathing. You should rarely notice their breathing unless you're specifically watching them.

> **QUICK TIP**
>
> *Know what's normal. Healthy hamsters eat, groom, and stay active during evening and night hours.*

Behavioral Health Signs

Active exploration during evening hours shows good health and mental stimulation. A healthy hamster displays curiosity about their environment, investigates new objects, and moves confidently around their space. This exploration should appear purposeful rather than frantic.

Regular grooming indicates comfort and well-being. Healthy hamsters spend considerable time cleaning themselves, following a systematic pattern from face to tail. This grooming should appear relaxed and thorough, not excessive or focused on one area.

Normal eating and drinking reflects good health and proper habitat conditions. A healthy hamster shows enthusiasm for food, maintains consistent eating schedules, and drinks water regularly. They should show interest in both regular food and appropriate treats.

Daily Health Monitoring

Morning check-ins help you notice changes early. Even though hamsters sleep during the day, a quick morning look can reveal whether they've eaten, used their wheel, and had normal activity overnight. Look for evidence of normal activity without disturbing their rest.

QUICK TIP
Sneezing isn't always sickness. Dusty bedding or drafts can cause sneezing — but it should stop quickly.

Evening observation during their active period provides the best opportunity to assess health. Watch for normal movement patterns, eating behaviors, and energy levels. This is when you're most likely to notice changes that might indicate developing health issues.

Weekly weight checks help track your hamster's overall health trends. Use a small digital scale to weigh your hamster weekly, recording the results in a simple log. Gradual weight changes are normal, but sudden gains or losses may indicate health problems.

Understanding your individual hamster's normal helps you distinguish between personality quirks and health concerns. Some hamsters are naturally more active or social than others. Learning your pet's normal personality helps you recognize when something changes.

7.2 Common Health Problems and Early Recognition

Understanding common health problems helps you spot issues early when treatment works best. While hamsters are generally hardy animals, certain conditions occur often enough that every owner should know their signs.

Respiratory Problems

Upper respiratory infections are among the most common health issues in hamsters. Early signs include slightly increased breathing rate, occasional sneezing, and minor nasal discharge. These symptoms can develop quickly into more serious conditions if left untreated.

Environmental causes often contribute to respiratory problems. Poor ventilation, ammonia buildup from dirty bedding, dusty bedding materials, or sudden temperature changes can all trigger respiratory issues. Addressing these environmental factors is often as important as medical treatment.

Serious signs that require immediate attention include labored breathing, mouth breathing, rattling sounds, or colored nasal discharge. These symptoms indicate the infection has progressed and requires prompt veterinary care.

Digestive Issues

Diarrhea can develop from dietary changes, stress, bacterial infections, or parasites. Early signs include softer than normal droppings, increased frequency, or slight changes in dropping color. Severe diarrhea can quickly lead to dehydration.

Wet tail is a serious bacterial infection that primarily affects young hamsters. Despite its name, it affects the entire digestive system and can be fatal if not treated promptly. Signs include diarrhea, lethargy, loss of appetite, and wetness around the tail area.

Skin and Fur Problems

Parasites including mites can cause intense itching, hair loss, and skin irritation. You may notice your hamster scratching excessively, developing bald patches, or showing signs of skin irritation.

Fungal infections can cause circular patches of hair loss, scaling, or crusty areas. These infections often start small but can spread rapidly if untreated.

Dental Problems

Overgrown teeth occur when hamsters don't have adequate chewing opportunities. Signs include difficulty eating, drooling, weight loss, or visible tooth overgrowth. This condition requires veterinary correction.

Prevention involves providing appropriate chewing materials like hard wooden chews and proper food textures to help maintain normal tooth length.

Injury Recognition

Limping or altered movement may indicate injuries from falls or accidents. Even minor limping should be taken seriously, as hamsters often hide pain effectively.

Swelling or lumps anywhere on the body require veterinary evaluation. While some lumps may be benign, others could indicate infections or other serious conditions.

7.3 Finding and Working with an Exotic Pet Veterinarian

Establishing a relationship with a qualified exotic pet veterinarian before you need emergency care is one of the most important steps in responsible hamster ownership. Not all veterinarians have experience with small mammals.

Choosing the Right Veterinarian

Exotic pet specialization is crucial for proper hamster care. Look for veterinarians who specifically list small mammals or exotic pets among their specialties. These professionals have additional training in the unique needs of hamsters and other small animals.

Experience matters when selecting a veterinarian. Ask about their experience with hamsters specifically, as techniques and medications that work for cats and dogs may not be appropriate for small mammals.

Facility evaluation helps ensure your chosen veterinarian can provide appropriate care. The clinic should have proper equipment for handling small animals and experience with exotic pet procedures.

Preparing for Veterinary Visits

Carrier preparation ensures safe transport. Use a small, secure carrier with

adequate ventilation and familiar bedding. Bring a small amount of your hamster's regular food in case the visit extends longer than expected.

Information gathering before your appointment helps maximize the visit's value. Prepare a list of questions, bring records of your hamster's weight and eating habits, and note any behavioral changes you've observed.

Understanding Treatment Options

Medication administration for hamsters requires special considerations due to their small size. Ask your veterinarian to demonstrate proper dosing techniques and discuss any potential side effects.

Cost considerations should include routine care costs and potential emergency expenses. Consider setting aside funds specifically for veterinary emergencies, or investigate pet insurance options that cover exotic animals.

7.4 Emergency Preparedness and First Aid

Medical emergencies can develop quickly in hamsters. Having a prepared response plan can make a significant difference. While first aid is never a substitute for professional veterinary care, knowing how to respond appropriately can help stabilize your hamster until professional help is available.

Recognizing True Emergencies

Breathing difficulties including labored breathing, mouth breathing, or blue-tinged gums require immediate veterinary attention. These symptoms can indicate serious respiratory infections, heart problems, or other life-threatening conditions.

Severe trauma from falls, crushing injuries, or accidents requires emergency care regardless of your hamster's apparent condition. Internal injuries may not be immediately obvious.

Neurological symptoms such as seizures, head tilting, loss of coordination, or unusual behavior patterns indicate serious problems requiring immediate professional attention.

Severe dehydration can develop quickly in hamsters. Signs include sunken eyes, dry mouth, skin that doesn't snap back when gently pinched, and lethargy.

Basic First Aid Principles

Stay calm and think clearly during emergencies. Your hamster will pick up on your stress, and panic can lead to poor decision-making.

Ensure safety for both you and your hamster before attempting any first aid. Remove immediate dangers and protect yourself from injury. An injured hamster may bite defensively.

Handle gently during emergencies. Injured hamsters may be more fragile than usual, and rough handling can worsen injuries. Use slow, deliberate movements and provide adequate support.

QUICK TIP
Sick hamsters may hide food. Sometimes they store food but don't eat it — a subtle sign they're not feeling well.

Control temperature to help prevent shock. Keep injured hamsters warm but not hot, using soft towels or your body heat. Avoid direct heat sources like heating pads.

Creating an Emergency Kit

Essential supplies include clean towels, a small carrier for transport, eyedropper for fluid administration, antiseptic solution, and emergency contact information. Keep these items easily accessible and check them regularly.

Emergency contacts should include your regular veterinarian, after-hours emergency clinics, and poison control resources. Program these numbers into your phone and keep written copies in your emergency kit.

Common Emergency Scenarios

Choking incidents may occur if hamsters eat inappropriate items. Signs include pawing at the mouth, difficulty breathing, and distress. Gentle examination of the mouth may reveal visible obstructions that can be carefully removed.

Heatstroke can develop rapidly in high temperatures. Signs include panting, lethargy, and loss of coordination. Move your hamster to a cooler location immediately and use cool (not cold) cloths to gradually reduce body temperature.

Poisoning symptoms vary but may include vomiting, diarrhea, difficulty breathing, or unusual behavior. If you suspect poisoning, remove any remaining toxic substance and contact your veterinarian immediately.

After-Hours Emergency Care

Preparation planning includes identifying 24-hour veterinary clinics that treat exotic pets and understanding their policies. Not all emergency clinics have exotic pet expertise.

Transportation during emergencies should keep your hamster warm, quiet, and secure. Avoid giving food or water unless specifically instructed by a veterinary professional.

7.5 Prevention: The Best Medicine

Preventing health problems is far more effective and less stressful than treating them after they develop. Most hamster health issues are preventable through proper care, environmental management, and attention to early warning signs.

Stress Reduction for Better Health

Environmental stability supports immune function and reduces susceptibility to illness. Maintain consistent temperature, lighting, and noise levels in your hamster's habitat. Sudden environmental changes can trigger stress responses that compromise health.

Routine maintenance of cleaning schedules, feeding times, and interaction patterns helps hamsters feel secure and reduces stress-related health problems. Predictable routines allow hamsters to relax and focus energy on maintaining health.

Respect individual personalities - some hamsters thrive with frequent interaction, while others prefer minimal handling. Forcing social interaction on reluctant hamsters creates stress that can manifest as health problems.

Proper Hygiene and Habitat Maintenance

Regular cleaning prevents the buildup of bacteria, ammonia, and other harmful substances that can cause illness. Consistent spot cleaning, weekly deep cleaning, and monthly thorough sanitization create healthy living conditions.

Bedding management involves choosing appropriate materials, maintaining proper depth, and changing bedding before it becomes contaminated. Poor bedding conditions contribute to respiratory problems and skin issues.

Food and water hygiene prevents bacterial growth that can cause digestive problems. Fresh water daily, clean food dishes, and prompt removal of perishable foods reduce disease risk significantly.

Exercise and Mental Stimulation

Physical activity requirements vary among individual hamsters, but all need opportunities for exercise to maintain cardiovascular health, muscle tone, and mental well-being. Provide appropriate wheels, climbing opportunities, and space for natural movement.

Mental enrichment prevents boredom and stress-related behaviors that can compromise health. Rotate toys, provide foraging opportunities, and offer appropriate challenges that engage your hamster's natural curiosity.

Environmental variety within safe parameters helps prevent behavioral problems and supports psychological health. Occasionally rearrange habitat features, introduce new safe materials, and provide seasonal enrichment opportunities.

Building Strong Immunity

Nutritional support through high-quality diet and consistent feeding schedules provides the foundation for strong immune function. Proper nutrition is the most important factor in preventing illness.

QUICK TIP
Check them daily. A quick daily check for clear eyes, clean fur, and normal behavior helps catch problems early.

Regular monitoring allows early detection of problems when they're most treatable. Weekly health checks, weight monitoring, and behavior observation help identify issues before they become serious.

Veterinary partnerships through regular check-ups and established relationships with exotic pet professionals provide support for maintaining optimal health.

Seasonal Health Considerations

Winter care may require attention to temperature stability and adequate nutrition as hamsters may eat slightly more in cooler weather.

Summer precautions include monitoring for heat stress and ensuring adequate ventilation and cooling options during warm weather.

Year-round vigilance helps you recognize that while seasonal changes may affect your hamster's behavior slightly, dramatic changes always warrant concern regardless of season.

Remember that you know your hamster better than anyone else. Trust your instincts—if something seems "off" even if you can't pinpoint exactly what, it's always appropriate to consult your veterinarian. Early intervention often leads to better outcomes and lower treatment costs.

....

Coming up in Chapter 8: Learn to establish sustainable daily, weekly, and monthly care routines that keep your hamster healthy while fitting into your family's busy schedule.

Chapter 8:
Daily, Weekly, and Monthly Care

8.1 Daily Care Routines That Work

Great hamster care doesn't have to take over your life! The secret is creating simple routines that become as automatic as brushing your teeth. When you build good habits from the start, taking care of your hamster feels natural instead of like a big chore.

Morning Check-In (5 Minutes)

Your hamster will probably be sleeping when you get up, but you can still learn a lot about how they're doing without waking them up.

Quick health check: Look around the habitat for signs your hamster had a good night. Did they eat some food? Is there evidence they used their wheel? You're basically being a detective, looking for clues that everything is normal.

Food and water check: See how much food disappeared overnight and whether the water level went down. If you left any fresh vegetables the night before, remove anything that looks wilted or old.

Spot any problems: Take a quick look for anything unusual—strange smells, damaged toys, or signs your hamster tried to escape. Most days everything will look fine, but catching problems early makes them much easier to fix.

Evening Interaction Time (10-15 Minutes)

This is when your hamster wakes up and gets ready to party! It's the perfect time for feeding, gentle handling, and just enjoying your pet's personality.

Work with their schedule: Most hamsters become active between 6-8 PM. Once you figure out your hamster's preferred wake-up time, try to do your main care tasks then. They'll be much happier and more cooperative when they're naturally awake.

Feeding routine: Give your hamster their daily food portion during this active time. Offer any fresh foods or healthy treats now too. Having a consistent feeding time helps your hamster know what to expect.

Social time: This is your best opportunity for gentle handling or just watching your hamster explore and play. Every hamster has their own personality - some love to climb on their owners, while others prefer to show off their acrobatic skills from inside their habitat.

Making Daily Care Work for Your Family

Share the responsibility: Different family members can handle different tasks based on their ages and schedules. Create simple checklists so everyone knows what to do.

Plan for busy days: Some days are crazier than others. Know which tasks are absolutely essential (fresh water, basic feeding) versus nice extras (extensive play time, habitat rearranging). Having a "minimum care day" plan prevents guilt when life gets hectic.

8.2 Weekly Deep Cleaning Made Simple

Once a week, your hamster's home needs a thorough refresh. This keeps them healthy and gives you a chance to really check how they're doing. With good planning, weekly cleaning becomes manageable and even satisfying.

QUICK TIP
Check the water bottle daily. Make sure it's full and not clogged — even one day without water can be dangerous.

Getting Ready (5 Minutes)

Gather your supplies first: Get everything ready before you start - fresh bedding, cleaning supplies, and a safe temporary space for your hamster. Having everything prepared makes the job go much faster.

Set up temporary housing: Your hamster needs a safe place to stay during cleaning. A secure travel carrier, small exercise pen, or backup habitat works perfectly. Make sure it has some bedding and maybe a favorite hideout to keep your hamster comfortable.

The Cleaning Process (20-30 Minutes)

Remove all bedding: Take out all the old bedding material. While you're doing this, notice if any areas seem extra dirty or have unusual odors - this can tell you about your hamster's bathroom habits or potential health issues.

Clean the habitat: Wash all removable parts with pet-safe cleaners. This includes food bowls, water bottles, exercise wheels, and hideouts. Avoid harsh chemicals that might leave dangerous residues.

Check equipment: While everything's apart, look for wear and tear. Check that wheels spin smoothly, examine toys for sharp edges, and make sure all habitat components are still secure and safe.

Fresh start: Add new bedding at least 6 inches deep so your hamster can burrow naturally.

Health Monitoring During Cleaning

Weekly weigh-in: Many families use cleaning time for a quick weight check. Use the same scale and time each week for the most accurate comparisons.

Physical check: When you handle your hamster for weighing or moving them, it's a good time to notice any changes in their coat, body shape, or movement that might need attention.

8.3 Monthly Health and Habitat Assessment

Once a month, take a step back and look at the big picture of your hamster's health and happiness. This deeper evaluation helps you spot gradual changes and plan for future needs.

Complete Health Review

Look for patterns: Compare your hamster's current behavior, appetite, and activity level to what you've observed over the past month. Gradual changes are often easier to spot when you look at longer time periods.

Activity evaluation: Has your hamster been using their wheel as much as usual? Are they climbing and exploring normally? Changes in exercise patterns can sometimes indicate developing health issues.

Environment Check-Up

How's the habitat working? Observe whether your hamster uses all areas of their home. Are there spots they avoid or areas they've claimed as favorites? This information helps you understand if any adjustments might improve their quality of life.

Equipment performance: Do a detailed inspection of all habitat components. Replace worn items before they break, and consider upgrading anything that isn't working as well as it should.

Planning and Budgeting

Supply inventory: Plan your next month's purchases to keep adequate supplies on hand. Buying bedding and food in reasonable quantities can save money while ensuring you never run out.

Emergency preparedness: Check that your first aid supplies are current and that you have up-to-date veterinary contact information.

FUN FACT
Clean cages = better behavior. A clean, enriched environment reduces boredom and stress-related chewing or bar-biting.

8.4 Seasonal Care Adjustments

Different seasons bring different challenges and opportunities for hamster care. Understanding these changes helps you keep your hamster comfortable year-round.

Spring and Summer

Activity increases: Many hamsters become more active as daylight hours increase. You might need to check exercise equipment more frequently.

Temperature control: During hot weather, provide cooling options like ceramic tiles and ensure good ventilation. Make sure fresh water is always available.

Food safety: Higher temperatures mean fresh foods spoil faster. Remove uneaten fresh vegetables more quickly.

Fall and Winter

Temperature stability: Monitor habitat temperatures closely during cold weather. Provide extra nesting

QUICK TIP

Keep a care checklist. A weekly or monthly log can help families stay on track with health and hygiene.

materials for comfort, but be careful not to make the habitat too hot.

Supply stocking: Take advantage of good weather to stock up on supplies before winter makes shopping more difficult.

Holiday planning: During busy holiday periods, plan ahead to ensure hamster care doesn't suffer. Assign specific responsibilities and arrange pet care for vacations well in advance.

Creating Your Seasonal Calendar

Monthly reminders: Create simple calendars noting seasonal tasks, supply needs, and health monitoring reminders. This helps you anticipate needs rather than scrambling to address them.

Family schedule integration: Plan hamster care routines that work with changing family schedules throughout the year, including school breaks and work changes.

Understanding these seasonal patterns helps you provide consistent, appropriate care throughout the year while preventing problems before they develop. These adjustments become routine with experience and contribute significantly to your hamster's long-term health and happiness.

· ·

Coming up in Chapter 9: Learn to identify and solve common behavioral challenges, environmental problems, and family situations that can arise during hamster ownership.

Chapter 9: When Problems Arise

9.1 Understanding Behavioral Challenges

Even the best-cared-for hamsters can sometimes develop behaviors that puzzle or worry their families. The good news? Most behavioral problems have simple explanations and solutions once you understand what your hamster is trying to tell you.

When Your Hamster Bites

Getting bitten by your hamster can be scary and disappointing, especially when you thought you were bonding well. But biting is almost always your hamster's way of saying "I'm scared" or "something hurts"—not "I don't like you."

Fear-based biting is the most common reason hamsters bite. When they feel cornered, startled, or threatened, their natural response is to defend themselves. This often happens when hamsters are handled too quickly, approached from above (which feels like a predator attack), or forced into interactions before they're ready.

Pain-related biting can develop when hamsters are experiencing illness or injury that isn't obvious to us. A normally gentle hamster who suddenly becomes defensive might be protecting a sore spot or dealing with internal discomfort.

Territorial biting occurs when hamsters feel their space or resources are threatened. This might happen during cage cleaning, when multiple people try to handle them quickly, or when they're eating.

How to help a biting hamster: First, stop all forced interactions immediately. Go back to basic trust-building - offer treats through the cage bars, talk softly to your hamster, and let them approach you voluntarily. Never punish or react dramatically to bites, as this confirms their fear that humans are dangerous.

QUICK TIP

Biting? Don't take it personally. Most biting comes from fear or surprise. Go slower, and try bonding with treats.

Prevention strategies: Learn to read your hamster's body language. Flattened ears, crouched posturing, or backing away all mean "give me space right now." Respecting these signals prevents most biting incidents.

Excessive Hiding and Shyness

Some hamsters are naturally more reserved, while others become shy due to stress or inadequate habitat setup. Both situations can improve with patience and the right approach.

New environment shyness is completely normal for the first few weeks after bringing your hamster home. They need time to feel safe in unfamiliar surroundings, and hiding is their natural way of coping with stress.

Inadequate security can cause ongoing hiding behavior. If your hamster's habitat doesn't have enough secure hiding spots or if it's too exposed, they may never feel safe enough to explore confidently.

Overstimulation from too much activity, noise, or interaction attempts can overwhelm sensitive hamsters. This is especially common in households with young children or in high-traffic areas.

Building confidence: Create a predictable, calm environment where your hamster can gradually build trust. Maintain consistent routines, speak softly around their habitat, and always let them choose whether to interact rather than pursuing them.

QUICK TIP
Spinning in circles or jumping at walls? This may be "cage stress." Upgrade their space and enrich the environment immediately.

Remember: Some hamsters are naturally more reserved than others, and that's perfectly okay! A shy hamster can still live a happy, healthy life with appropriate care for their personality.

Destructive or Repetitive Behaviors

When hamsters engage in unusual behaviors like excessive bar chewing, obsessive wheel running, or aggressive bedding manipulation, they're usually telling you something about their environment or stress level.

Bar chewing often signals boredom, stress, or habitat problems. While some light chewing is normal, constant bar chewing can damage teeth and usually means your hamster needs more mental stimulation or space.

Excessive wheel running beyond normal exercise might indicate stress or lack of other enrichment options. While wheel running is healthy, non-stop running without breaks can signal underlying issues.

Solutions that often help: Increase habitat complexity with additional hiding spots, climbing opportunities, and foraging challenges. Make sure your hamster has adequate space and bedding depth for natural behaviors. Consider whether environmental factors like noise, lighting, or temperature might be causing stress.

Sleep Disruption and Noise Concerns

Hamsters are naturally active at night, which can create challenges for families who need quiet sleep. Understanding this natural pattern helps you find solutions that work for everyone.

Normal vs. problematic activity: All hamsters will be most active during human sleep hours—this is completely natural and healthy. However, excessive noise from faulty equipment or stress-related behaviors can be addressed.

Practical solutions: Position habitats away from bedrooms when possible, choose quieter exercise wheels, secure toys properly to prevent rattling, and ensure all equipment is well-maintained.

Family strategies: Help household members understand that nighttime activity is normal hamster behavior. White noise machines, closed bedroom doors, and realistic expectations can improve everyone's sleep quality.

9.2 Environmental and Habitat Solutions

Environmental problems can develop gradually or appear suddenly, but most are solvable with some detective work and practical adjustments.

Managing Odor Issues

While some hamster odor is normal, persistent or strong smells usually indicate problems that can be fixed.

Understanding normal odors: Healthy hamsters have a mild, musky scent that shouldn't be overpowering. Normal habitat odors come mainly from urine and scent marking—both natural behaviors.

When odors become problematic: Strong ammonia smells, persistent unusual odors, or smells that cleaning doesn't improve might indicate health issues, inadequate ventilation, or cleaning routine problems.

Practical solutions: Improve air circulation around the habitat, ensure adequate cleaning frequency without overdoing it (which can increase stress), choose bedding materials that absorb odors effectively, and spot-clean high-use areas more frequently.

Health-related concerns: If cleaning and environmental improvements don't resolve persistent odors, consult your veterinarian. Unusual smells can sometimes indicate urinary tract infections or other health issues.

Preventing and Handling Escapes

Most hamster escapes are preventable with proper habitat security and regular maintenance.

Common escape routes: Loose-fitting lids, worn door latches, damaged habitat walls, or gaps between components are the usual culprits. Regular inspections help you spot and fix problems before they lead to escapes.

If your hamster escapes: Stay calm and use recovery techniques that encourage voluntary return. Place familiar food, bedding, and hideouts near the habitat. Keep the area quiet so your hamster feels safe enough to come out of hiding.

Temperature and Environmental Control

Hamsters are sensitive to temperature extremes, but most environmental problems are manageable with awareness and preparation.

Heat stress prevention: During summer or in warm areas, provide cooling options like ceramic tiles, ensure good ventilation, and watch for signs of overheating like lethargy or rapid breathing.

Cold weather care: Maintain appropriate temperatures without creating fire hazards. Provide extra nesting materials, eliminate drafts, and consider safe supplemental heating if needed.

Space and Territory Issues

Recognizing space problems: Signs that your hamster might need more space include excessive bar chewing, repetitive pacing, unused areas of the habitat, or aggressive behavior during handling.

> **QUICK TIP**
> Make care a family habit. Assign daily tasks like feeding, checking water, and spot-cleaning to build responsibility.

Practical improvements: While ideal habitat sizes are generous, work within your family's space and budget constraints. Focus on making existing space more interesting with vertical climbing options, varied textures, and enrichment activities.

9.3 Family and Social Dynamics

Changes in family circumstances, disagreements about care, and evolving relationships with pets create challenges that affect both hamster welfare and family harmony.

Helping Children Develop Responsibility

Set realistic expectations: Match care responsibilities to children's developmental abilities. A 10-year-old can handle daily feeding and basic observation, while complex health monitoring might need adult supervision.

Build skills gradually: Start with simple, concrete tasks and add complexity as children demonstrate reliability. This builds confidence and prevents overwhelm that can lead to giving up.

Maintain motivation: Children's interest in pet care naturally fluctuates, especially during busy school periods or when the novelty wears off. This is normal! Have backup plans that ensure your hamster's welfare without creating guilt or conflict.

Managing Family Member Allergies

Identify the real culprits: Reactions might come from the hamster, bedding materials, food dust, or cleaning products. Accurate identification helps you choose the most effective solutions.

Practical management strategies: Air filtration, bedding changes, modified cleaning routines, and limited exposure protocols can often allow families to keep their hamsters even with mild allergies.

When professional help is needed: If allergies are severe or don't improve with environmental changes, consult with both your family doctor and veterinarian about options.

Vacation and Travel Planning

Local care arrangements: Professional pet sitters, trusted friends, or family members usually provide the best care for hamsters during family absences. Provide detailed but simple care instructions and emergency contact information.

Extended absence planning: Longer trips require more comprehensive arrangements and detailed care protocols. Plan these well in advance to ensure your hamster's welfare throughout extended periods.

When Family Situations Change

Moving considerations: Plan moves carefully to minimize stress for your hamster. Prepare the new habitat area in advance, transport safely, and re-establish routines quickly in the new location.

Financial changes: If money becomes tight, focus on essential care needs first—adequate food, clean water, basic habitat maintenance. Many hamster care costs can be managed with planning and smart shopping.

> **Understanding Your Limits**
>
> **Behavioral problems:** If consistent, patient efforts don't improve aggressive behavior, severe anxiety, or dangerous behaviors within a reasonable time, professional consultation can provide new strategies and insights.
>
> **Health concerns:** While basic monitoring and first aid are important owner skills, diagnosing and treating health problems requires veterinary training. When in doubt, consult your vet rather than guessing.
>
> **Environmental challenges:** Persistent problems like ongoing odors, recurring escapes, or habitat issues that don't respond to basic solutions might need expert advice or significant changes.

9.4 Knowing When to Seek Help

Recognizing when problems are beyond your ability to solve prevents minor issues from becoming serious while ensuring your hamster gets appropriate professional care when needed.

Finding Local Resources

Hamster communities: Online forums and local pet groups provide valuable support, advice, and resource sharing. Experienced hamster owners often offer practical solutions based on their own experiences.

Veterinary care: Establish a relationship with a veterinarian experienced with small mammals before you need emergency care. Ask friends, local pet stores, or online communities for recommendations.

Making Difficult Decisions

Quality of life considerations: Sometimes you need to evaluate whether current arrangements truly serve your hamster's best interests. Consider physical health, behavioral wellbeing, and environmental adequacy honestly.

When rehoming might be necessary: Major family changes, severe allergies, or care requirements that exceed your family's capabilities might make rehoming the most responsible choice. Focus on finding appropriate new homes rather than quick solutions.

Financial reality: Balance your desire to provide optimal care with your family's financial constraints. Focus on essential needs first, and don't feel guilty about making practical choices within your means.

Remember that seeking help isn't a sign of failure—it's responsible pet ownership! Professional support, community resources, and expert guidance complement good basic care to ensure the best outcomes for both you and your hamster.

Most problems that arise in hamster ownership are solvable with patience, understanding, and the right approach. The key is recognizing that challenges are normal parts of pet ownership, not signs that you're doing something wrong.

Coming up in Chapter 10: Learn about your hamster's life stages, planning for end-of-life care, and considering future hamster relationships as your experience grows.

Chapter 10: Growing Together

10.1 Your Hamster's Life Journey

Understanding your hamster's journey through different life stages helps you provide the best care while preparing emotionally for the natural changes that come with aging. Each stage brings its own joys and challenges.

Baby and Young Hamster Stage (0-4 months)

Amazing growth happens fast: Baby hamsters change from tiny, helpless creatures to active, curious young hamsters in just a few weeks. If you adopt a very young hamster, you'll be amazed by how quickly they develop new skills and personality traits.

Extra nutritional needs: Growing hamsters need more protein and calories than adults. They also need constant food availability because their small size makes them more vulnerable to going without food for too long.

Prime socialization time: Gentle, consistent interaction during these early

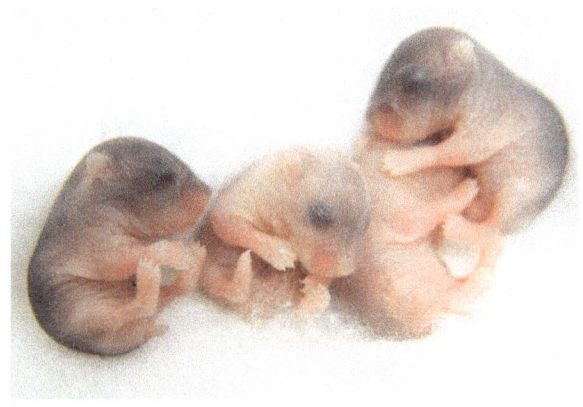

months helps develop confident, well-adjusted adult hamsters who are comfortable with human contact. This is when your hamster learns whether humans are friends or threats.

Extra care needed: Young hamsters are more sensitive to temperature changes, stress, and handling mistakes. A little extra patience during this period prevents problems that might affect them throughout their lives.

Adult Prime Years (4-18 months)

Peak performance time: This is when hamsters are at their healthiest, most active, and most interactive. Many families find this the most rewarding period of hamster ownership because their pet's personality really shines through.

Personality becomes clear: During adult years, your hamster's individual traits and preferences become obvious. Some are natural athletes, others are architects who love rearranging their bedding, and many are little comedians with unique quirks.

QUICK TIP

Adults need routine. Stable feeding times, consistent cage layout, and regular interaction help adult hamsters thrive.

Building your relationship: The bonds formed during this period often provide the most emotional rewards of hamster ownership. Your hamster learns to recognize your voice, may come to greet you, and develops trust in your care.

Early Senior Stage (18-24 months)

Gradual changes begin: Your hamster might start sleeping a bit more, moving slightly slower, or showing minor changes in appetite. These changes often happen so slowly that they're barely noticeable at first.

Mobility adjustments might help: If your hamster seems to have trouble reaching favorite spots, consider providing easier access to food, water, and resting areas. Simple modifications can maintain their quality of life.

Health monitoring becomes more important: While you shouldn't become overly worried, keeping a closer eye on eating, drinking, and activity patterns helps catch any developing issues early.

Advanced Senior Care (24+ months)

More noticeable changes: As hamsters reach advanced age, changes in activity, appetite, or mobility may become more apparent. These reflect natural aging processes, not poor care on your part.

QUICK TIP
Adjust handling over time. Older hamsters may prefer shorter, gentler bonding sessions. Let them set the pace.

Focus on comfort: The goal shifts from optimal performance to maintaining dignity, comfort, and quality of life. Your hamster may need softer bedding, warmer areas, or modified habitat arrangements.

Quality time becomes precious: Senior hamsters often become more affectionate and content to spend quiet time with their families. These gentle interactions can be deeply meaningful for both you and your pet.

10.2 Expanding Your Knowledge and Community

Growing as a hamster owner means continuing to learn and connecting with other people who share your interest in these amazing animals. This journey enriches your experience while helping hamsters everywhere.

Continuing Your Education

Advanced topics: As you gain experience, you might want to learn about specialized nutrition, advanced environmental enrichment, or deeper understanding of hamster behavior. This knowledge helps you provide exceptional care.

Stay current: Small mammal care continues to evolve as researchers learn more about what hamsters need to thrive. Following reputable sources helps you stay updated on best practices.

Document your journey: Keeping track of what you learn helps you remember important information and creates a reference for future use. Your experiences become valuable knowledge to share with others.

Joining the Hamster Community

Local connections: Finding other hamster enthusiasts in your area provides face-to-face support, opportunities to see different care approaches, and friendships based on shared interests.

Online communities: Quality online groups offer broader perspectives, access to experts worldwide, and support available whenever you need help or want to share experiences.

Share your knowledge: As you gain experience, answering questions and mentoring new owners helps build stronger communities while reinforcing your own learning. Teaching others often deepens understanding.

10.3 When It's Time to Say Goodbye

Planning for your hamster's end of life is one of the hardest parts of pet ownership. However, thinking about these issues ahead of time helps ensure that final decisions reflect love and your hamster's best interests rather than panic or guilt.

Recognizing Quality of Life Changes

Physical comfort signs: Watch for changes in your hamster's ability to move around comfortably, eat and drink normally, or perform basic grooming. Difficulty with these essential activities can indicate declining quality of life.

Behavioral changes: Loss of interest in normal activities, withdrawal from interaction, disrupted sleep patterns, or inability to perform natural behaviors like exploring might signal declining comfort or health.

Appetite and weight: While some fluctuation is normal with aging, persistent loss of interest in food or significant weight loss may indicate discomfort that affects quality of life.

Making Compassionate Decisions

Veterinary guidance: Professional assessment helps you understand what your hamster is experiencing and what to expect. Experienced small mammal veterinarians can help you make informed decisions about care options.

Family discussions: End-of-life decisions should reflect the values and agreement of all family members involved in your hamster's care. Children need age-appropriate involvement and support through this process.

QUICK TIP
Prepare for goodbye with kindness. When a hamster reaches the end of its life, gentle care and comfort are the best gifts you can give.

Quality vs. quantity: Sometimes the most loving decision involves preventing suffering rather than extending life as long as possible. Focus on your hamster's comfort and dignity rather than simply buying more time.

Honoring Your Hamster's Memory

Celebrating your relationship: Focus on the joy, learning, and love your hamster brought to your family rather than dwelling only on sadness. Photo collections, memory books, or simple ceremonies help process grief while honoring your pet's impact.

Understanding grief: Losing a beloved pet creates real sadness that deserves recognition. This is especially important for children, who need help understanding that grief over pet loss is normal and valid.

Creating positive legacies: Consider donations to animal welfare organizations, sharing your knowledge with other families, or volunteering to help other hamsters in need. These actions create positive outcomes from your loss.

10.4 Considering Your Next Hamster

Deciding whether and when to welcome another hamster requires careful consideration of emotional readiness, practical circumstances, and lessons learned from your experience.

Timing Your Decision

Emotional readiness varies: Family members process grief differently and may feel ready for new relationships at different times. Some people benefit from new companionship quickly, while others need extended time to heal.

Family agreement matters: Decisions about new pets should reflect everyone's feelings rather than pressure from some family members. Children

especially need their emotions respected during these decisions.

Learning integration: Consider what worked well with your previous hamster, what you might change, and how your knowledge and skills have developed. This experience makes you a better caregiver for future pets.

Applying Your Experience

Improved care opportunities: Your experience creates confidence and knowledge that benefit new pets significantly. You understand hamster needs, can recognize health issues earlier, and know how to create enriching environments.

Realistic expectations: Previous experience helps you understand individual hamster personalities, interaction patterns, and bonding processes. This knowledge prevents disappointment while helping you appreciate each hamster's unique qualities.

Building on Your Journey

Mentoring opportunities: Experienced families can help newcomers avoid common mistakes while sharing the joy and knowledge that comes from successful hamster ownership.

Community involvement: Share experiences, support fellow owners, and advocate for proper care standards to help improve welfare for hamsters everywhere.

Continued learning: Each hamster relationship offers new lessons and opportunities for growth as caregivers and animal advocates. Every pet teaches something different.

Your Hamster Journey Continues

Your experience with hamsters represents more than just caring for small pets. It's an opportunity to develop compassion, responsibility, and appreciation for animals while creating cherished family memories. Each hamster you welcome contributes to your growth as caregivers while benefiting from the love, knowledge, and commitment you provide.

The skills you develop, relationships you build, and knowledge you gain through hamster ownership often influence other areas of life, creating positive effects that extend far beyond pet care. Whether you choose to welcome one hamster or many throughout your life, each relationship offers unique rewards and learning opportunities.

Great hamster ownership combines scientific knowledge with compassionate care, creating experiences that teach responsibility while providing years of joy and companionship. You now have the tools and understanding to provide exceptional care throughout your hamster's entire life while building meaningful relationships that benefit both your family and your pet.

Remember that every hamster deserves a family that approaches their care with knowledge, patience, and love. By reading this book and taking hamster ownership seriously, you're already demonstrating the kind of thoughtful, responsible approach that leads to wonderful experiences for both pets and families.

🩺 Quick Reference & Emergency Guide

Emergency Contacts (Fill In!)

Primary Vet: _____ **Phone:** _____

Emergency Vet: _____ **Phone:** _____

Backup Caregiver: _____ **Phone:** _____

Poison Control: _____

Call Vet IMMEDIATELY If:

- **Breathing:** Difficulty breathing, wheezing, mouth breathing
- **Injury:** Bleeding, limping, swelling, eye damage
- **Neurological:** Seizures, loss of balance, head tilt, unresponsive
- **Digestive:** Bloody diarrhea, no eating/drinking 24+ hours, bloating
- **Other:** Significant weight loss, extreme temperature, discharge

Basic First Aid (Get Vet Care Too!)

- **Minor Cuts:** Clean gently, apply pressure, keep warm, call vet
- **Poisoning:** Remove from source, DON'T induce vomiting, save sample, go to vet
- **Overheating:** Move to cool area, provide cool water, damp cloth nearby, call vet
- **Choking:** Check mouth gently, hold head down, gentle back pressure, go to vet

Normal vs. Concerning Behavior

NORMAL (Don't Panic)	CONCERNING (Monitor)	URGENT (Call Vet)
Sleeping during day	Reduced activity for days	No appetite 24+ hours
Active at night	Eating/drinking changes	Difficulty moving
Stuffing cheeks	Constant scratching	Labored breathing
Hiding when startled	New aggression	Seizures
Cage cleaning fussiness	Repetitive behaviors	Severe diarrhea

Quick Daily Health Check (30 seconds)

- **Eyes:** Clear and bright?
- **Breathing:** Quiet and regular?
- **Movement:** Walking normally?
- **Appetite:** Evidence of eating?
- **Alert:** Responds to you?

Emergency Kit Essentials

- Small towels and carrier
- Heating pad (low setting)
- Eye dropper
- Vet's phone number
- Digital scale
- This guide

Key Reminders

✅ **DO:** Stay calm, handle gently, take notes, trust your instincts

❌ **DON'T:** Give human meds, force food/water, wait with serious symptoms

Remember: You know your hamster best. If something seems off, call your vet!

INDEX

A
accessories, 24–25, 25–26
activity levels, 30
activity patterns, 40–41
adjustment period, 33–36
adult hamsters, 29, 93
age considerations, 29
allergies, 89
animal shelters, 30
apples, 50
aquarium tanks, 19
Aspen shavings, 21
avocado, 51

B
bar chewing, 85, 88
beans, 51
bedding, 14, 21, 75
behavioral challenges, 83–86, 90
biting, 83–84
destructive behaviors, 85
hiding and shyness, 84–85
noise, 86
repetitive behaviors, 85
sleep disruption, 86
behavioral health signs, 29, 67–68
bell peppers, 49
berries, 49
bin cages, 19–20
biting, 83–84
body language, 37–39
body weight, 67
bonding, 59–61
breathing, 67
breathing difficulties, 72
breeders, 30
budgeting, 81
bulk purchasing, 26
burrowing, 41–42

C
cages. *See* habitats
Campbell's dwarf hamsters, 12
care routines
daily, 77–79
monthly, 80–81
seasonal adjustments, 81–82
weekly, 79–80
chicken, 50
children, developing responsibility in, 88
chocolate, 51
choking, 73
cinnamon hamsters, 12
citrus fruits, 52
cleaning routine, 75, 79–80
climate control, 23–24
coat, 67, 69–70
commercial food, 47
commitment check, 13–14
communication, 43–45
costs of ownership, 15

D
daily care routines, 77–79
daily health monitoring, 68
daily routines, 39–41
dairy products, 52
dangerous foods, 51–53
defensive hamsters, 58
defensive postures, 38
dehydration, 72
dental problems, 70
destructive behaviors, 85
diabetes, 55
diarrhea, 69
digestive problems, 52, 55, 69
drinking patterns, 68
dwarf hamsters, 12–13, 14, 19, 30

E

ears, 38
eating patterns, 68
eggs, 50
emergency contacts, 73
emergency kits, 73
emergency preparedness, 53, 72–74, 81
end-of-life issues, 95–96
enrichment, 24–26, 50–51, 63, 64, 75
environmental control, 87–88
environmental problems, 86–87, 90
escapes, 87
essential items checklist, 25
evening observation, 68, 78
exercise, 75
exercise wheels, 11, 22, 25
exploration, 37–38, 63–65, 67
eyes, 66

F

fall, 81–82
family dynamics, 88–90
family readiness assessment, 15–17
family situations, changing, 89
fear indicators, 38–39
feeding
    hand, 59–60
    schedule, 41, 48, 78
financial considerations, 15, 89, 91
first aid, 72–73
fish, 52
food, 25
    commercial, 47
    dangerous, 51–53
    foraging and enrichment, 50–51
    fresh, 48–50
    hygiene, 75
    toxic, 51
    treats, 48–50
    in wild vs. captivity, 46
food hoarding, 42
food poisoning, 53, 73
food storage, 23, 42
foraging, 50–51, 63
fruits, 49–50, 52
fungal infections, 70
fur problems, 69–70

G

garlic, 51
golden hamsters, 12
grapes, 51
grooming, 42–43, 67–68
growth monitoring, 54

H

habitats
    budget-friendly options, 27
    choosing right size, 18–19, 21
    cleaning routine, 75, 79–80
    lighting and ventilation, 24
    maintenance of, 75
    monthly check of, 80–81
    options for, 18–20
    preparing for arrival, 32–33
    requirements for, 14
    temperature and climate control, 23–24
    toys and accesories for, 24–25
hair loss, 69–70
hamster community, 95
hamsters
    body language, 37–39
    choosing, 13, 28–30
    communication by, 43–45
    considering next hamster, 96–98
    feeding, 46–55
    introduction to, 9–11
    life stages of, 92–94
    natural behaviors of, 39–43
    reputable sources for, 30–32
    safe handling techniques, 56–59
    types of, 11–13
hand feeding, 59–60
handling techniques, 56–59
health indicators, 28–30, 35–36, 39, 66–68

health monitoring, 68, 80
health problems, 68–70, 90
    preventing, 74–76
heatstroke, 73
help, knowing when to seek, 90–91
hemp bedding, 21
hiding, 84–85
hiding spots, 22, 26
hoarding, 42
holding position, 57
housing options, 14, 18–20, 27

I
iceberg lettuce, 52
illness indicators, 39
immunity, 76
injury recognition, 70
interactions, first, 34–35
itching, 69

J
juvenile nutrition, 54, 92

L
leafy greens, 49
lifespan, 15
life stages, 92–94
lifting technique, 57
lighting, 24
limping, 70
litter training, 62
local resources, 90, 95
lumps, 70

M
meat, 52
medication administration, 71
mental stimulation, 24–25, 75–76
money-saving strategies, 26
monthly care routine, 80–81
morning check-ins, 68, 77–78
moving, 89

N
name recognition, 62
natural behaviors, 39–43
nervous hamsters, 58
nesting, 41–42
neurological systems, 72
noise concerns, 86
nose, 66–67
nutrition, 46–51, 53–55
    for good health, 76
    juvenile, 54, 92
    senior, 54

O
obstacle courses, 63
odor issues, 86–87
onions, 51
online communities, 95
overgrown teeth, 70

P
pain signals, 39
panda hamsters, 12
paper bedding, 21
parasites, 69
pears, 50
personlity types, 58
pet carrier, 32
pet loss, 96
pet stores, 30
physical health, 28, 66–67
play areas, 63–64
poisoning, 53, 73
portion control, 48
potatoes, 51
pregnancy, 54
processed foods, 52, 52–53
protein, 50
puzzle feeders, 50–51

R
raisins, 51

readiness assessment, 15–17
red flags, 29, 31–32
rehoming, 90
repetitive behaviors, 85
requesting behavior, 44
respiratory problems, 69
response training, 62
Roborovski hamsters, 12
root vegetables, 49
routine development, 34, 59

S
scatter feeding, 50
scratching, 69
seasonal care adjustments, 81–82
seasonal health considerations, 76
senior hamsters, 29, 54, 58, 93–94
settling in period, 33–36
setup costs, 15, 27
shopping tips, 25–26
shy hamsters, 58, 84–85
skin problems, 69–70
sleep disruption, 86
sneezing, 68
social engagement, 38
solitary nature, 13
space issues, 88
space needs, 14, 18–19, 21
special dietary considerations, 53–55
spring, 81
stress indicators, 38–39, 43–44, 59
stress reduction, 74–75
summer care, 76, 81, 87–88
supervision techniques, 64
supplies, 14, 25–26
swelling, 70
Syrian hamsters, 11–12, 13, 14, 18, 30

T
teddy bear hamsters, 12
teeth, 70
temperature control, 23–24, 87–88
time commitment, 13–14

toxic foods, 51
toys, 24–25, 63
training, 61–63
transporting home, 32
trauma, 72
travel planning, 89
travel tips, 32
trust building, 35, 59–61
trust indicators, 44
turkey, 50

U
upper respiratory infections, 69

V
vacation planning, 89
vegetables, 49
ventilation, 24
vet
    finding and working with, 70–72, 90
    partnership with, 76
    visits to, 71–72
    when to call, 35
vocal communication, 43–44
voice tone, 61

W
warning signs, 39
water systems, 23, 75
weekly care routine, 79–80
week one, 33–36
weight check-ins, 68
wet tail, 69
wheel running, 85
winter care, 76, 81–82, 88
winter white dwarf hamsters, 12

Y
young hamsters, 29, 54, 92–93

www.ingramcontent.com/pod-product-compliance
Lightning Source LLC
Chambersburg PA
CBHW082211070526
44585CB00020B/2370